MW00582017

JUNG STRIPPED BARE BY HIS BIOGRAPHERS, EVEN

JUNG STRIPPED BARE BY HIS BIOGRAPHERS, EVEN

Sonu Shamdasani

KARNAC

LONDON   NEW YORK

First published in 2005 by
H. Karnac (Books) Ltd.
6 Pembroke Buildings, London NW10 6RE

Copyright © 2005 Sonu Shamdasani

The right of Sonu Shamdasani to be identified as the author of this work
has been asserted in accordance with §§ 77 and 78 of the Copyright Design
and Patents Act 1988.

All rights reserved. No part of this publication may be reproduced, stored
in a retrieval system, or transmitted, in any form or by any means,
electronic, mechanical, photocopying, recording, or otherwise, without the
prior written permission of the publisher.

Cover photograph of Jung by Ximena Roelli

British Library Cataloguing in Publication Data

A C.I.P. for this book is available from the British Library

ISBN 1 85575 317 0

Edited, designed and produced by The Studio Publishing Services Ltd,
Exeter EX4 8JN

Printed in Great Britain

10 9 8 7 6 5 4 3 2 1

www.karnacbooks.com

CONTENTS

ACKNOWLEDGEMENTS   ix

Introduction: Biography, fiction, history   1

CHAPTER ONE
"How to catch the bird": Jung and his first biographers   9

CHAPTER TWO
The incomplete works of Jung   47

CHAPTER THREE
Other lives   59

CHAPTER FOUR
A new Life of Jung   87

Conclusion: Life after biography?   117

REFERENCES   119

INDEX   127

For Maggie

ACKNOWLEDGEMENTS

In a recent work, *Jung and the Making of Modern Psychology: The Dream of a Science*, I sought to study the constitution of Jung's psychology, within the context of the formation of psychology, psychotherapy, and the human sciences, largely on the basis of a study of primary materials. While it reconstructed aspects of the reception of Jung's works in his lifetime, it did not consider the plethora of secondary literature that has arisen since his death. This book takes up this latter question, through reconstructing the history of Jung's biographies and the editing of his works. I would like to thank Brett Kahr, who proposed this project to Oliver Rathbone at Karnac Books, Oliver himself for his enthusiastic response and support of the project, and also Leena Häkkinen at Karnac Books, for seeing it swiftly through the publication process. My thanks also go to Tonya Curry, Alan Elms, Ulrich Hoerni, Max Fordham, the late Michael Fordham, Emmanuel Kennedy, Andreas Jung, the late Franz Jung, Peter Jung, Steve Martin, David Quentin, Ximena Roelli, and Gudrun Seel for their assistance. In my work I have attempted to bring to bear a contemporary historical approach to the field of Jung, and have been assisted by numerous colleagues and friends at work in the history of psychology, psychiatry, and psychoanalysis. In particular, I am indebted to Mikkel Borch-Jacobsen, Ernst Falzeder, Angela Graf-Nold, George Makari, Richard Skues, Anthony Stadlen, Peter Swales, and Eugene Taylor for their parallel endeavours in Freud and Jung history. Likewise, I would like to thank my colleagues at the Wellcome Trust Centre for the History of Medicine at UCL for the continued example of exemplary historical work on a regular basis. I am grateful to Niedieck Linder AG and the Erbengemeinschaft C. G. Jung for permission to cite from Jung's unpublished correspondences, and Ximena Roelli for permission to cite her correspondence and that of Cary Baynes. Responsibility for the views expressed here is my own.

Introduction: biography, fiction, history

"Nothing would have prevented it," said Jung. "I mean—imagine! A man tries to kill himself with a spoon. Sounds like a fair desperation to me. I had nothing to do with it.

"You curried favour with him. The minute you held the jacket for him he knew he had you in the palm of his hand. I despair. You did this with Blavinskeya. You raved about the wonders of the Moon. You did it with the Dog-man. You allowed his minder to walk him on a chain. You told the Man-with-the-imaginary-pen you thought he had created the most beautiful writing you had ever read! I swear you don't want to bring them back. You want to leave them stranded in their dreams!"

Jung turned towards the bureau and fingered a photograph there in a silver frame. It showed a woman who appeared to be in mourning—eyes cast down, chin lowered, black beads and dress.

"It isn't true," he said, "that I want to abandon them to their dreams. But someone has to tell them their dreams are real." Then he added: "and their nightmares."

"They aren't real. They're what they are—the manifestations of madness."

1

"The Moon is real," Jung said. "A dog's life is real. The imagined word is real. If they believe these things, then so must we . . . at least until we have learned to talk their languages and hear their voices."

This conversation between C. G. Jung and Dr Fürtwangler did not take place. Neither the patients—the Dog-Man, the Man-with-the-imaginary-pen, Blavinskeya nor Dr Fürtwangler himself, ever existed. The dialogue occurs in *Pilgrim*, a novel by Timothy Findlay, which presents the imaginary encounter between "pilgrim", a man who can never die, and Jung, whom he meets when he is placed in the Burghölzli in 1912.[1] Jung had actually left the Burghölzli in 1909, but this conceit enabled Findlay to imagine how "Jung" may have reacted to the extraordinary fate of such an individual, had such events occurred. To flesh out his account, Findlay drew from historical information concerning Jung which he wove together with his fantasy, liberally inventing scenes that never took place, some of which, nevertheless, as in the account above, may have some plausibility, given the historical Jung's insistence on the psychic reality of fantasies, and the importance of taking delusions seriously. In the context of a novel, such elaborations are entirely legitimate. But history is a quite different enterprise.

Findlay's novel is not the first work, nor is it likely to be last, in which Jung is featured in a fictional context. What is it about him that attracts such fictions? Why does he attract the interest of novelists and playwrights? One answer to these questions may be found in the plasticity of contemporary images of Jung. In cultural discourse, his name is often evoked to denote a whole host of cultural, religious, philosophical, political, and psychological issues as a kind of shorthand. Discussions that appear to be ostensibly about him may, on closer examination, carry scant relation to historical actuality.

As a result of this, we are faced today with a serious predicament. Currently, vast sectors of the public are unable to distinguish between fictionalized accounts of Jung from the historical figure, due to the myths, fictions, and errors that abound in the profusion of literature about him. Alarmingly, professional Jungians are not

---

1. Findlay, 1999, p. 57.

immune to this. This situation is compounded by the dearth of reliable historical and biographical information about him and the insufficiently realized fact that many manuscripts, seminars, and thousands of letters still remain unpublished.

How did this situation arise, and what can be done to remedy it? One answer may be found through tracing the history of attempts to provide biographical accounts of Jung's life, and to assess how successful they have been. Before doing so, we may consider some general aspects of how Jung has been understood.

Freud and Jung have been widely seen as the founders of psychotherapy and modern depth psychology. Such a perspective presents a particular view of the type of fields that these are: rather than being seen as disciplines which emerge from complex developments in Western thought and society, spanning many disciplines and involving many figures, psychotherapy and depth psychology have been seen as the solitary creations of Freud and Jung. These creation myths of psychotherapy have in turn had important legitimating functions for the very identity of these fields.

During the past few decades a number of scholars have been presenting radically different accounts of the genesis of these disciplines. Recently, I presented a new account of the genesis of Jung's psychology, coupled with a new account of aspects of the rise of modern psychology and psychotherapy.[2] This work challenged what may be called the "Jungian legend". Significant aspects of this may be summarized as follows: that Freud was the founder of psychotherapy; that Jung was a disciple of Freud and derived his ideas from him; that the two most important figures for Jung in the genesis of his work were Freud and Spielrein; that after his break with Freud, Jung had a breakdown and from this analytical psychology arose; that during this "confrontation with the unconscious" he discovered (or invented) his ideas of the collective unconscious, archetypes and individuation; that analytical psychology represents a revision of psychoanalysis; that Jung wrote an autobiography, which has been taken as the main source of information about his life and work; and that analytical psychology today directly descends from Jung, and, indeed, was founded by him.

---

2. Shamdasani, 2003.

In this form, the Jungian legend is in part a tributary to what has been called the "Freudian legend". The main elements of this are the claims that psychoanalysis has had a wide impact on twentieth century society, and has led to wide scale transformations in social life; that Freud discovered the unconscious; that Freud was the first to study dreams and discover their meaning; that Freud was the first to study sexuality, discover infantile sexuality, and his discoveries provoked a storm of disapproval due to Victorian repression; that Freud invented modern psychotherapy, and psychoanalysis was the most advanced form of psychotherapy; that these discoveries were based on his self-analysis and observation of patients. In the past four decades of Freud studies, under the critical scrutiny of Freud historians, this legend has died a death. Yet somehow, in general discourse, the legend still lives on.[3]

These legends served to telescope intellectual history into a "great men" view of history, and to reduce the history of psychoanalysis and analytical psychology into a battle between solitary geniuses. On the one hand, these legends perform a function of radical dehistoricization: Freud and Jung are deracinated from their social and intellectual contexts, as founders of universal theories. On the other, these legends serve to legitimate contemporary discourses, and function as convenient creation myths. Thus, the names of Freud and Jung are frequently invoked to authorize conceptions and practices which have no necessary connection to their own.

The success of these legends has also been aided by two particular styles of thought. The first is what Mikkel Borch-Jacobsen and I have called "interprefaction", which designates a key trait of psychoanalytic thinking: interprefaction signifies the manner in which interpretations and constructions are treated as facts. When interprefaction prevails, the requirement of evidence recedes. Due in part to the impact of psychoanalytic thinking on biography, interprefaction has come to play a critical role in biographies, and has led to loose forms of psychobiography. In such works, elements from the historical record are woven into narratives based on

---

3. On the Freudian legend, see Henri Ellenberger (1970a, pp. 547–548), Frank Sulloway (1979, pp. 489–495), and Mikkel Borch-Jacobsen and Sonu Shamdasani, forthcoming.

psychodynamic models. Psychoanalytic interpretation fills in the gaps of the historical record, and where it encounters obstacles, events and occurrences are simply resignified to fit into a pre-given frame, through a series of symbolic equivalences in which anything can stand in for anything else. The plot of a life is supplied by a ready-made, off-the-shelf theory.

The second style of thought is the valorization of a subjectivist conception of truth. In this, it is held that each individual has their "own" Freud or Jung, and that this is "psychically real" and has as much validity as anyone else's Freud or Jung. In some variants, this is allied to forms of radical perspectivalism derived from dubious readings of post-structuralist thought.[4] However useful such a conception may be in psychotherapy, when applied to history it has deleterious consequences. As historical figures, Freud and Jung become cancelled out, and one can say whatever one likes about them. All views are treated as opinions on an equal level, and history, as a discipline, is negated.

Within this context, biography comes to play a particular role. "We've become a culture of biography", noted Justin Kaplan in 1994, likening the "saturating presence of biography" to "an invasion of the body snatchers".[5]

In the introduction to a recent volume on scientific biography, Michael Shortland and Richard Yeo remarked on the paradox that whilst we are in an "Age of Biography", and while surveys show biographies to be the most popular form of non-fiction in Britain, biography remains the one of the "least studied forms of contemporary writing."[6] Two issues they comment on pose particular problems for history: the erosion of the distinction between biographies and novels, and how little many biographers draw upon the work of historians.[7] Thus, for the general public, the historical landscape is more likely to be configured by biographers than by historians.

This is particularly marked in the cases of Freud and Jung. Given the vast expanse of their oeuvres and the mountains of

---

4. For examples, Christopher Hauke, 2000; Susan Rowland, 1999, 2002.
5. Justin Kaplan, 1994, pp. 1, 8.
6. Shortland and Yeo, 1996, p. 1.
7. *Ibid.*, pp. 3–4.

secondary literature about them, individuals turn to biographies to provide the key to an understanding of their life and work. New biographies of Jung—unlike new works by Jung—are widely reviewed in newspapers and periodicals, and sell better than his works. Thus, we live in a time in which such biographies play a critical role in shaping the public perception and reception of his work. Consequently, contemporary images of Jung owe more to biographies than to any other genre. In such a context, it is all the more critical that biographies be historically accurate.

In the case of Jung, the attraction of biographies is increased by the difficulty of some of his writings. In 1946, he wrote to Wilfred Lay:

> You have understood my purposes indeed, even down to my "erudite" style. As a matter of fact it was my intention to write in such a way that fools get scared and only true scholars and seekers can enjoy its reading.[8]

Thus, biographies of Jung offer the promise of rendering his work more accessible, particularly to general readers.

Biographies of psychologists also serve to humanize them. Mundane details of day to day activities and "all too human" incidents serve to bring them closer, and function as a compensation for the larger than life mythic status that they have obtained. Since psychologists have proposed new ways of living, one seeks to investigate their lives to see how they lived and embodied their own psychology, and also to see how their particular idiosyncrasies may have shaped their psychologies. Thus, biographies play a critical role as a tool to evaluate their works, and function as informal types of "psychology criticism".

In biographies of psychologists, the use of formal or informal modes of psychological interpretation by biographers is often particularly problematic. The tenets of a particular school of psychology, or the biographer's home-made psychology are all too often taken as universal accounts of character and motivation, superior to those of the psychologist in question. Thus, biographies may serve to legitimate particular pre-existing interpretations,

---

8.   20 April 1946, in Adler, 1973, p. 425.

perspectives and prejudices, through embedding these within the narration of a life.

Thus the "life" genre provides a frame that gives permanence to a particular reading of Jung. Such a perspective risks short-circuiting the complex task of evaluating a multi-faceted work. By turning to biography to provide an account of the genesis of a psychology, biography becomes a substitute, ersatz history. Thus, rather than evaluating Jung's work in connection with past and present developments in psychiatry, psychology, psychotherapy, the human sciences, comparative religion, theology, and so on, opinions concerning his personal conduct in real or imagined circumstances all too easily form the ultimate locus of judgement.[9]

There have been many biographies of Jung, spanning half a century. Thus, Jung biographies form a subdiscipline unto themselves. But have they brought us fundamentally nearer the historical Jung? Can any of these lay claim to be definitive? How should one view their contradictory accounts? This work sets out to address these questions. It commences with a consideration of Jung's views on biographies and autobiographies, and follows the attempts to write biographical works on Jung during his lifetime by Lucy Heyer, E. A. Bennet and Aniela Jaffé. It traces the vicissitudes of the publication of Jung's *Collected Works*, and indicates the unsuspected consequences this has had for subsequent biographies and works on Jung. It considers the biographical projects of Barbara Hannah, Vincent Brome, Gene Nameche and R. D. Laing, Paul Stern, Gerhard Wehr, Frank McLynn, Ronald Hayman, and Deirdre Bair. Finally, it asks: how many posthumous lives does Jung have to live?

---

9.   One may contrast this with Nietzsche's admonition concerning the evaluation of the works of artists in *The Genealogy of Morals*: "one does best to separate an artist from his work, not taking him as seriously as his work. He is, after all, only the precondition of his work, the womb, the soil, sometimes the dung and manure on which, out of which, it grows—and therefore in most cases something one must forget if one is to enjoy the work itself" (Nietzsche, 1887, II, 4).

CHAPTER ONE

"How to catch the bird":
Jung and his first biographers

In the history of modern psychology, psychiatry and psychotherapy, a number of prominent figures wrote memoirs or autobiographies: such as Auguste Forel, Stanley Hall, Emil Kraepelin, and Wilhelm Wundt. In the field of psychoanalysis, Freud, Ernst Jones, and Wilhelm Stekel published autobiographical works. In the 1930s, the American psychologist Carl Murchison edited a series of volumes entitled *A History of Psychology in Autobiography*, in which he managed to get important psychologists such as Édouard Claparède, Pierre Janet, William McDougall, Jean Piaget, William Stern, J. B. Watson, and many others to write autobiographical contributions. Murchison began his book by noting: "The author of a recent history of psychology found that it was impossible to get facts concerning the scientific development of certain individuals except from those individuals themselves."[10] Thus, for the history of psychology to be possible, some form of biographical research was unavoidable. In different ways, these

---

10. Murchison, 1930a/1960, p. ix. Murchison did not approach Jung for this, but he had asked Jung to contribute to his volume, *Psychologies of 1930*

accounts showed how psychologists could use their own life stories as important tools to establish their accounts of the genesis of their works, to further their own estimations of their historical significance, and to settle scores with their rivals and competitors. At the same time, such autobiographies presented formidable obstacles to any attempt to establish unbiased historical accounts of the genesis of their works.

Within this context, there was from early on great interest in Jung's life story.[11] The closest he came to presenting any of it in public was in a seminar held at the Psychological Club in Zürich in 1925. Notes of these seminars were taken by Cary de Angulo (later Baynes).[12] He commenced these seminars by stating to his audience, "I would like to give you a brief sketch of the development of my own conceptions from the time I first became interested in problems of the unconscious."[13] This encapsulates Jung's perspective: his interest was to give an account of the development of his *conceptions*, and he only spoke of his personal experience in so far as it illuminated this. At the same time, Jung made it clear what he was not saying. In speaking about the genesis of his work on psychological typology, he commented:

> All of this is the outside picture of the development of my book on the types. I could perfectly well say that this is the way the book came about and make and end of it there. But there is another side. A weaving about making mistakes, impure thinking, etc., etc., which is always very difficult for a man to make public. He likes to

---

(Murchison 1930b). Jung had declined, recommending his assistant H. G. Baynes instead (Murchison to Jung, 2 November 1928, Jung archives, Eidgenössische Technische Hochschule (Swiss Federal Institute of Technology), Zürich, [hereafter, JA]).

11.   This chapter draws upon material presented in Shamdasani 1995 and 2000.

12.   Unlike some of his later seminars, these were checked by Jung, and can be taken as reliable. On 19 October 1925, Jung wrote to Cary de Angulo, "I faithfully worked through the Notes as you will see. I think they are as a whole very accurate. Certain lectures are even fluent, namely those where you could not hinder your libido from flowing." (Original in English, Baynes papers—hereafter, BP). Unless otherwise noted, unpublished Jung letters are in German, and translations are my own.

13.   Jung, 1925, p. 3.

give you the finished product of his directed thinking and have you understand that so it was born in his mind, free of weakness. A thinking man's attitude towards his intellectual life is quite comparable to that of woman toward her erotic life.

If I ask a woman about the man she has married, "How did this come about?" she will say, "I met him and loved him, and that is all." She will conceal most carefully all the little meannesses, and squinting situations that she may have been involved in, and she will present you with an unrivalled perfection of smoothness. Above all she will conceal the erotic mistakes she has made . . .

Just so with a man about his books. He does not want to tell of the secret alliances, the *faux pas* of his mind. This it is that makes lies of most autobiographies. Just as sexuality is in women largely unconscious, so it is this inferior side of his thinking largely unconscious in man. And just as a woman erects her stronghold of power in her sexuality, and will not give away any of the secrets of its weak side, so a man centers his power in his thinking and proposes to hold it as a solid front against the public, particularly against other men. He thinks if he tells the truth in this field it is equivalent to turning over the keys of his citadel to the enemy.[14]

In this remarkable statement, what Jung sees as the near impossibility of honesty, which "makes lies of most autobiographies", proves to be the major contraindication for entering upon such an endeavour. Clearly, Jung hadn't the slightest intention of "turning over the keys of his citadel" to his enemies.

In the years following this seminar, Jung consistently held to this position. In 1953, Henri Flournoy, the son of Jung's mentor, the Swiss psychologist, Théodore Flournoy, relayed to Jung the question of a Dr Junod as to whether he had written an autobiography, or intended to do one.[15] Jung replied: "I have always mistrusted an autobiography because one can never tell the truth. In so far as one is truthful, or believes one is truthful, it is an illusion, or of bad taste."[16] In a letter to his lifelong friend Gustave Steiner, Jung

---

14. *Ibid.*, pp. 32–33.
15. Henri Flournoy to Jung, 8 February, 1953, JA.
16. Jung to Henri Flournoy, (Adler, 1975, p. 106, original in French, tr. mod.). In a dedicatory note to a collection of his offprints for Jürg Fierz, Jung simply wrote: "I myself have a distaste for autobiography." 21 December, 1945, in Adler, 1973, p. 404.

expressed his continued resistance to undertaking an autobiography, despite concerted pressure:

> During the last years it has been suggested to me on several occasions to give something like an autobiography of myself. I have been unable to conceive of anything of the sort. I know too many autobiographies and their self-deceptions and expedient lies, and I know too much about the impossibility of self description, to give myself over to an attempt in this respect.[17]

Jung was no less sanguine concerning the possibility of a biography of his life. In reply to J. M. Thorburn, who had suggested that Jung should commission a biography of his life, Jung replied:

> if I where you I shouldn't bother about my biography. I don't want to write one, because quite apart from the lack of motive I wouldn't know how to set about it. Much less can I see how anybody else could disentangle this monstrous Gordian knot of fatality, denseness, and aspirations and what-not! Anybody who would try such an adventure ought to analyze me far beyond my own head if he wants to make a real job of it.[18]

In 1954, Jung gave an interview to Cleonie Carroll Wadsworth, in which he commented on his suitability as the subject for a biography:

> Someone wants to write my biography but it is foolish. I am a simple Bourgeois. I seldom travel—I sit here and write or walk down my garden—my life has not been dramatic. Now old Schweitzer is dramatic—playing the organ, working in a long white coat among the palm trees or going with the bible under his arm to preach—or healing people. No one knows what I am doing and it is not paintable and you cannot take a picture of it.[19]

This raises the question, what representational conventions would be suitable to depict the life of someone dedicated to the exploration of inner events?

---

17.   30 December, 1957, in Adler, 1975, p. 406, tr. mod.
18.   6 February, 1952, *ibid.*, pp. 38–39.
19.   1 March 1954, Countway Library of Medicine, Harvard Medical School (hereafter, CLM).

Jung's resistance to writing an autobiography or having a biography of him written didn't stop others from pressing him on both of these points.

A biography of C. G. Jung

In the same period, Jung was entering into a retrospective phase. On 2 January 1949, he wrote to Alwina von Keller, "I also find myself at this time in a retrospective phase and am occupied again fundamentally with myself for the first time for 25 years, in that I collected and put together my old dreams."[20]

In 1952, Lucy Heyer, the wife of Gustav Heyer proposed a biography of Jung, which was to be published by Daniel Brody of Rhein Verlag. She intended to base her work on extended interviews with Jung, which would set it apart from all other works on him.[21] Initially, she had proposed to collaborate with Cary Baynes on the biography.[22] On 5 September, 1952, her daughter Ximena de Angulo wrote to Cary Baynes about this project after a conversation with Jung:

> By this time you have received my letter saying that C. G. distinctly told me that he didn't care to have Lucy undertake this alone, but only in collaboration with you. It would have of course been better if he could have made Brody understand this clearly; just why he didn't, I couldn't say. When I realized that Brody and Lucy were under the illusion that she was acceptable to him alone, I didn't feel it was my place to correct this impression. . . . He [Jung] very definitely wants you to undertake it. . . . C. G. said he didn't see why you should have such doubts and fears as to your competence, that you had done the 1925 Notes admirably, and he visualized this as a sort of amplification of that technique. He said that in itself the idea of a biography gave him a certain discomfort, that he certainly would never write an autobiography (as he also said in Bollingen two

---

20. JA.
21. On 25 July 1951, Lucy Heyer sent Jung a synopsis in five chapters (JA).
22. Bair noted that Jung asked Cary Baynes to write his biography in the 1930s, without citing a source (Bair, 2003, p. 585) There is no mention in their correspondence of this.

years ago, when I questioned him on your behalf) but that he realized that circumstances were making it necessary. I had the impression that he would very much like that it be done in a way that he
could control, so no nonsense would issue, not by some nincom-
poop after his death. I asked him if the interview method you had
thought of would not be very tiring for him, and he said, oh no, that
wouldn't be so bad, that he could do it quite well.[23]

This indicates that in Jung's conception, the project would be 'an
amplification' of the 1925 seminar, and that the factor which was
overcoming his aversion to a biographical enterprise was the
increasing realization that someone was bound to undertake one
anyway. Ximena de Angulo tried to persuade her mother to collaborate with Lucy Heyer, indicating that in her view, Lucy Heyer was
too much in awe of Jung, her feelings were hurt too easily and she
was insufficiently conversant with his ideas.[24] She added that Jung
had indicated that he thought that Lucy Heyer did not know him
well. On 26 September, Ximena de Angulo wrote again to her
mother:

> I think there is a real danger of an outsider horning in, Jung seemed
> to imply that when he said to me that he saw the time had come to
> have a project of this sort undertaken. Reporters are constantly now
> to interview him, and it wont be long before some enterprising
> person saw the chance of a book being got out on him.[25]

Lucy Heyer requested funding from the Bollingen Foundation,
indicating that she intended to write it in collaboration with Cary
Baynes.

On 6 January 1953, Olga Froebe-Kapteyn informed Jack Barrett
of the Bollingen Foundation that Jung had agreed to Lucy Heyer's
undertaking. She added that Cary Baynes had a completely different idea of a work on Jung, and written to Lucy Heyer to do her
project on her own.[26] As the Foundation had stopped funding new
projects of this sort, Paul Mellon, who started it, agreed to directly

---

23. BP.
24. *Ibid.*
25. BP.
26. Bollingen Archive, Library of Congress (hereafter, BA).

support the project out of his own funds. Lucy Heyer received a grant of $5,000 over two years.[27] On 7 October, Jung wrote to Cary Baynes on the matter:

> Concerning the great plan for a biography, I want to tell you that although I fully agree with Lucy Heyer as the right person to do it, I have insisted from the beginning that you should come in. You represent an entirely different point of view which is presumably rather important. At all events, I would like you to join in and collaborate with Mrs. Heyer, and you had better hurry up before I am getting altogether too senile![28]

For Jung, the participation of Cary Baynes was essential to the project.

Meanwhile, Lucy Heyer presented the following outline of her biography:

SUGGESTIONS towards a BIOGRAPHY of C. G. JUNG

It should be an account of the origin and development of his work; a picture of the process in which Jung's ideas were born and matured; of the sources from which they drew their nourishment; of the historical periods and ancestors or forerunners that definitely determined Jung's unfoldment and of the traditions he has taken over and to which he has given continuity.

In so far as Jung's origin and descent, the atmosphere of family and landscape, education, school, university and profession were influential and therefore important as factors in the growth of his personality, they will be included in the biographical study, but only to the degree in which they have helped to form the man and his work. The same may be said of his contacts with people, countries and the various forms and history of culture.

The greatest stress however will be laid upon the origin and the formulation of his most decisive discoveries, In these an age-old western inheritance, such as that of Gnosis and Alchemy, has been regenerated. But in these revelations we also see the consummation

---

27. Paul Mellon to Lucy Heyer, 14 April 1953, BA.
28. BP, original in English.

of syntheses, conceived of in creative vision, which are only just beginning to take shape in the concrete world, in a historical and sociological aspect: the synthesis of East and West in a spiritual and intellectual sense.

Great and creative individuals serve as a reflector for those perceptions and realisations which are ahead of their time and which receive their valid imprint through an inner-creative act of such an individual. Jung has achieved this in great measure for our times. His personality can therefore not be shown without including those manifesting and hidden forces that weave the pattern of our epoch.

A further task of this book would consist in revealing the various paths by which the thoughts and ideas of antiquity and of the middle ages, as well as the wisdom of the East flowed into Jung's mind, into his sphere of thought, impregnating and extending it. This task demands an examination of the role played in Jung's development by authors of the 19th and 20th century, the philosophers, (for ex. Kant, Schopenhauer, Nietzsche) the psychologists, (French, English, German schools) and poets (Goethe, the romantic poets).

Thirdly it would be necessary to show how Jung's discoveries, realisations and formulations already affect his own time, how they have not only fertilized theory and practice of Depth-Psychology, but also that of other sciences, and what impulses radiate from his work to the world of today. This part of the study will have to remain fragmentary because these effects have only just begun to be apparent and their scope cannot be foreseen.

For the compilation of this material, in addition to that of the literature and the historical sources, Jung's own evidence must be taken into account. The book would have to be written in continual contact with him and would represent a distillation of extensive personal interviews on all important questions. It should be an "authorized" book and would therefore differ from all other publications relating to Jung's psychology, either as reviews or critical studies. In contrast to those representations which already exist, the book we conceive of would not treat Jung's work from a systemic, but rather from a dynamic point of view—a longitudinal section— and would thereby constitute a valid biography.

Lucy Heyer-Grote

CONTENTS OF THE BIOGRAPHY OF C. G. JUNG

(Provisional. The final formulation and sequence will develop from the interviews with C. G. Jung.)

Part I. Life history.

Origin.—Ancestors.—Parents and home.—Schools and University.—Profession.—Travels.—Important contacts with contemporary scholars. (Burckhardt, Freud, Bleuler, Wilhelm, Zimmer and others.)

Part II. Chronological development of Jung's Complex Psychology in its separate elements.

The TYPES.

The COLLECTIVE UNCONSCIOUS and the ARCHETYPES.

Research into SYMBOLS. (DREAMS: in Antiquity.—in the FAR EAST.—in early Christianity.—in Alchemy.—in Primitive Symbolism.)

PSYCHIC ENERGY AND LIBIDO.

Part III. The spiritual and intellectual "Fathers" of Jung.

Antiquity: The Pre-Socratics. Plato.

Middle Ages: Plotin.—Augustine.—Church Fathers.—Paracelsus.—The Alchemists.

Modern Times: Goethe.—Carus.—Romantic poets.—Kant.—Nietzsche.—Schopenhauer.—Dubois.—Janet and many others.

Part IV. C. G. Jung's influence on our times.

In MEDICINE and PSYCHIATRY.

In other sciences.

In Literature and Art.

Pupils.—Successors.—Opponents.[29]

---

29. Translated by Olga Froebe-Kapteyn, BA.

While undoubtedly reverential in tone, and presenting Jung as a world historical individual, the projected work nevertheless proposed a comprehensive contextual location of Jung's work in Western intellectual history and its contemporary reception.

Jung's support of Heyer's project was decisive for the Bollingen Foundation's wish to financially support her project. In a letter to Jung, Cary Baynes expressed some reservations concerning Lucy Heyer's philosophical approach. He replied:

> After many long initiating ceremonies, Lucie Heyer has settled down in Basel and has now begun in earnest. I have given her a book about Freud by Ernest Jones so that she gets an idea of the stuff that is talked about me. You need not be afraid: I shall try my best to stamp out every attempt to make of me a philosopher.[30]

He ended the letter by remarking: "I am curious to see how Lucie Heyer is going to proceed: I still don't see exactly how she is planning to catch the bird."[31]

Writing to Paul Mellon, Lucy Heyer expressed her satisfaction with the progress of the biography: "Prof. Jung has shown great interest in the work and is most willing to give me all the information I need."[32] However, Jung had increasing reservations concerning Lucy Heyer, and her appropriateness for the task. In addition, his qualms concerning the possibility of a biography had not receded. On 4 April, 1954, he wrote to Cary Baynes:

> Concerning our dear Lucy Heyer I get more and more the feeling that you have left me holding the baby. She would like to see me at least once a week, so that I could produce a biography for her. I have tried to produce some flies for her to catch, but I don't know whether she got anywhere with that game. I must say I never would have thought of helping somebody as far away as Lucy Heyer to write my biography. You just muscled her in, and I, thinking she might alleviate your task, said yes, and you just faded out. I'm quite unable to continue this funny kind of playing at a biography. You could just as well ask me to help that foolish American

---

30.   30 November 1953, BP, orig. in English.
31.   28 March 1954, BA, orig. in English.
32.   BA.

Radio-Company to produce myself in the form of a film.[33] I don't go to church on Sundays with a prayer-book under my arm, nor do I wear a white coat, nor do I build hospitals, nor do I sit at the organ. So I'm not fodder for the average sentimental needs of the general public. And that will be so with my biography. There is just nothing very interesting in it.[34]

Cary Baynes' reply sheds an interesting light on the genesis of the project:

It has taken me a long time to figure out why you thought I had "muscled" Lucy Heyer into the situation and then left you "holding the baby" . . . Brody was the person who did the muscle work and it was a *fait accompli* before I knew the subject had been broached. From her letter to me, August 1952, it was clear that Lucy thought she had a mandate to write the book, to write it with me if possible, but if I could not collaborate, still to write it by herself.

Later on I heard from Ximena that you definitely wanted me in the picture. I then wrote you via Emma—you were ill at the time—and gave you some of the reasons why it was unlikely that I would be able to collaborate with Lucy. I enclosed with this letter a copy of the one I had received from Lucy and called Emma's attention to the fact that if further misunderstandings were to be avoided, Brody and Lucy would have to be told where they had got off the beam. This is what I said; "Will he clear up this confusion introduced by Brody? That is, will he write Brody that he does not want Lucy to go it alone? I think it will take a direct word from him to settle the matter."

This word was never sent to Brody and so, Lucy, after she had heard definitely from me that I could not collaborate, went on happily thinking that the mandate held as she had understood it. Hearing nothing to the contrary, I too concluded that you were willing for her to do the book by herself. I honestly thought that she was capable of doing the kind of biography she had outlined.

---

33. Notwithstanding this comment, Jung subsequently consented to several filmed interviews: an interview with Stephen Black in July 1955, a portion of which was broadcast on *Panorama*; in August 1957, an lengthy interview with Richard Evans, and in October 1959, an interview with John Freeman for his *Face to Face* programme.

34. BP, orig. in English.

However, if Lucy wears you out, and feel she is too far away from you for you to be able to talk to her, that is positive proof that she is incapable of doing the biography. I don't think you would have this feeling about her if she had not shown herself to be obtuse. Obviously she cannot cure herself of obtuseness at this point of history, but equally obviously, you don't have to endure it. The best thing you can do now is to break off with her on the score of health. It is a perfectly valid reason. I talked about this with Jack Barrett before he left, and he was in hearty agreement. He said you need not have any hesitation on the financial side, because she is not on a grant, but is being financed by a personal contribution from Paul Mellon. Jack said too, that neither he nor Paul would want to be party to anything that drains your strength.[35]

On 9 September, Jung wrote to Cary Baynes, "in all the interviews I have had with her so far, I found nothing from which I could conclude that she would be capable of producing something that would look like an intelligent biography. I must say, I am for a biography, an utterly uninteresting case, so I don't wonder that she doesn't get anywhere."[36]

On 28 September, Lucy Heyer wrote to Barrett requesting further funds to complete her work. She gave as the reason for her delay the fact that the speed of the book depended upon Jung's health and readiness to grant her interviews. As an example of the work she had completed, she stated that she had written a chapter demonstrating that Jung's notion of psychic energy was "rooted in an experience of Jung's childhood, and how it grew and developed throughout his writings."[37] On 16 November, Barrett wrote to Jung informing him of Heyer's request. He added that Mellon was willing to add a year or two of funding, but that he (Barrett) wanted first to know if Jung thought this was advisable.[38] Jung's reply is revealing in terms of his attitude to the project, and indicates a less than enthusiastic response to the work she had done:

Up to the present, I haven't seen a line of what she has written about my biography. A while ago, I told her it would be nice to see

---

35. 4 August 1954, BP.
36. BP, orig. in English.
37. BA.
38. BA.

once something of all the interviews I had given her. But up to now I have seen nothing. I am not sure at all whether she has worked out something or not. I always wondered what she was going to do about her interviews, but I couldn't say that I have got any idea of it. You will understand that under these circumstances I have grown progressively less keen to entertain the dear old lady and I have regretted the loss of time rather precious to me. Thus, if I may express my view of the situation, I shouldn't weep many tears if somebody would lead the sad lady kindly away. I must say with my limited imagination I cannot conceive how she could possibly construct a biography of myself, but not being a literary man I would hardly know how to go about in writing a biography.[39]

On this basis, Mellon decided to provide a "modest sum" to see her to the end of 1955, to enable her to put into shape the material she had collected. A few months later, however, Jung had decided to terminate the project. Heyer had sent Jung a manuscript, and he replied on 2 February, 1955:

My decision in no way indicates a negative judgement on your intelligence or your ability, but springs entirely alone from my understanding, that in my case the abyss between my damned obligations and duty is really terrible. This would make me completely discouraged, if I entrusted myself with such a task.[40]

On 24 March, he wrote to Cary Baynes: "I have stopped my biographical interviews with Mrs. Heyer; it took too much time and too little has come from it. She doesn't have the necessary push."[41] In an undated letter to Daniel Brody which appears to be an explanation for the termination of the project, Jung wrote:

I have gained the impression from what I have read that my life does not at all contain the matter from which one could make a biography worth reading. I feared this from the beginning and for that reason also never could imagine, how one would be capable of externalising a plausible image of a life [Lebensbild] from a long chain of banalities and inconspicuous things.[42]

---

39. 24 November 1954, BA, orig. in English.
40. JA.
41. BA, orig. in English.
42. JA.

It is unclear how much of her work projected work she actually completed and the nature of her interviews with Jung. The withdrawal of his support effectively stopped the project altogether.

An 'Eckerfrau'

Meanwhile, the legendary publisher Kurt Wolff had unsuccessfully tried to get Jung to write an autobiography for years. In the summer of 1956, he suggested a new project to Jung at the Eranos conference, along the lines of Eckermann's *Conversations with Goethe*. Jolande Jacobi proposed Aniela Jaffé for the task, because, as Jung's secretary, it would be easier for her to ask questions concerning his life in free hours.[43] In the autumn, Kurt Wolff wrote to Aniela Jaffé,

> I feel it would be most desirable to present the material in a very direct way, Eckermann-like, or rather, giving Jung's memories of people, places, and events in his own words in the first person singular "as told to Aniela Jaffe".[44]

A few months later, he wrote to her that

> Let us by all means avoid for ourselves the word and idea of a "biography." After all, the whole idea of the book is that it should not be a biography, but as nearly as possible an autobiography.[45]

At that time, Jung already had exclusive contracts with Routledge and Kegan Paul and the Bollingen Foundation. That another publisher managed to publish Jung's "autobiography" was quite a coup, though clearly one that Kurt Wolff was up for. In an article entitled "On luring away authors, or how authors and publishers part company", Wolff wrote:

---

43.   Aniela Jaffé, draft foreword to *Memories*, Rascher archives, Zentral-bibliothek, Zürich (hereafter RZ), p. 1. On the composition of *Memories*, see also Alan Elms, 1994.

44.   24 Oct 1956. Beineke library, Yale University (hereafter, BL).

45.   16 January 1957, BL.

Every country in the world has strict laws about white-slave traffic. Authors, on the other hand, are an unprotected species and must look after themselves. They can be bought and sold, like girls for the white-slave trade—except that in the case of authors it is not illegal.[46]

To Richard Hull, Jung's translator, Kurt Wolff described how:

for several years he had tried to persuade Jung to write it [an auto-biography], how Jung had always refused, and how finally he (Kurt) hit on the happy idea of an "Eckerfrau" to whom Jung could dictate at random, the Eckerfrau being Aniela Jaffé.[47]

In a letter to Herbert Read, Kurt Wolff wrote that in the last analysis it was Aniela Jaffé who persuaded Jung to undertake this task.[48] An early provisional title was 'Carl Gustav Jung's Improvised Memories'. It was to be presented in the first person.[49] For Kurt Wolff, the work was not intended for Jungians, but for general readers. He hoped that it would be a book which would "lead the outsider inside the work".[50]

Due to the involvement of another publisher, the book did not go down the same editorial channels as the rest of Jung's work, which was to have significant consequences for what ensued. Like Lucy Heyer, Jaffé undertook a series of regular interviews with Jung, which she noted in shorthand. These notes were later typed out. Copies of the notes of these interviews are currently in the Library of Congress in Washington and at the ETH in Zurich (hereafter

---

46.   In Ermarth, 1991, p. 21.
47.   Richard Hull, "A record of events preceding the publication of Jung's autobiography, as seen by R. F. C. Hull", 27 July 1960, BA. The Eckermann–Goethe analogy was not lost on Jung; in a letter to Kurt Wolff, he wrote "God help me, when I read Eckermann's *Conversations* even Goethe seemed to me like a strutting turkey-cock" 1 February 1958, in Adler, 1975, p. 453).
48.   27 October 27 1959, BA.
49.   On 2 January 1957, Kurt Wolff drew Jaffé's attention to a work by Paul Claudel entitled *Mémoires improvisés* (1954), BL. This consisted of a series of broadcast interviews by Jean Amrouche in which he questioned Claudel on his life. The dialogical form of the interviews is clearly preserved in the published version.
50.   Kurt Wolff to Cary Baynes, 18 Sept 1959, BP ("dass die outsider inside the work fuehrt").

referred to as the "protocols").[51] Jaffé referred to these interviews as
her "biography hours".[52] In these interviews, Jung spoke about a
wide range of subjects. Jaffé, with the close involvement of Kurt
Wolff, selected material from these interviews and arranged them
thematically. This was then organized into a series of approximately
chronological chapters. To Kurt Wolff, Jaffé indicated that she
intended to focus on "Jung and Nature: Inner and outer". That is, his
relation to dreams and everything connected to them on the one
side, and on the other, to the earth.[53] When Jaffé started sending
Kurt Wolff the protocols of her interviews with Jung, he was very
impressed by them, and thought that they should be edited as little
as possible.[54]

In her introduction to *Memories* Aniela Jaffé wrote:

> We began in the spring of 1957. It had been proposed that the book
> be written not as a "biography" but in the form of an "autobiogra-
> phy", with Jung himself as the narrator. This plan determined the
> form of the book, and my first task consisted solely in asking ques-
> tions and noting down Jung's replies.[55]

She added that the genesis of the work determined its eventual
form. Hence a word or two is necessary concerning Aniela Jaffé and
her relationship with Jung. Jaffé first encountered Jung in 1937, and
subsequently went into analysis with him. Twenty years later,
she became his secretary. It was a job she was well suited to, as she
had already worked as a freelance secretary for Professors Gideon
and von Tscharner.[56] In 1947 she became secretary of the Jung
Institute.

---

51. This copy of the protocols was donated by Helen Wolff to Princeton
University Press, who in turn donated them to the Library of Congress in 1983,
placing a ten year restriction on them. I studied these in 1991, and they have
been on open access since 1993. Bair stated that the copy in the Library of
Congress, which is in the Bollingen collection, is restricted (2003, p. 657, n. 7).
This is actually unrestricted and was moved to a separate collection. The copy
at the ETH in Zürich is restricted.
52. "Biographie-Stunden", Jaffé to Kurt Wolff, 10 January 1958, BL.
53. Jaffé to Kurt Wolff, 11 January 1957, BL.
54. Kurt Wolff to Jaffé, 28 May 1957, BL.
55. Jung/Jaffé, 1962, p. 7.
56. CLM, p. 11.

In an interview with Gene Nameche, she recalled that after his wife's death, Jung did not feel like answering his correspondence, and that she answered many letters in his name, reading him her replies, to which he at times made minor corrections.[57] This working arrangement shows the initial level of trust that Jung showed in Jaffé, allowing her to "write in his name." It further helps us understand how *Memories* was composed. At the outset, Jung trusted her ability to "assume his 'I'", and to represent it to the outer world. For Jaffé, the project was supremely important. She informed Alwina von Keller that she regarded her role as the "catalyser" in it as the most fundamental one in her life.[58]

At the beginning of the project, Jung wrote a letter to Jaffé giving her permission to publish her notes of her conversations with him, and to supplement these with excerpts from autobiographical notes which he had made, such as the *Red Book*, the *Black Books*, his Africa diary, his "Impressions from a trip through India", and the 1925 seminar.[59] Thus, Jaffé had extensive primary materials at her disposal.

During the composition of the work there were many disagreements between the parties involved, concerning what the book should contain, its structure, the relative weighting of Jung and Jaffé's contributions, the title, and the question of authorship. There were also legal wrangles between the publishers involved as to who held the rights of the book.

In 1958, Jung decided to write a memoir of his early recollections, a number of which he had already relayed to Aniela Jaffé in her interviews.[60] Jaffé informed Kurt Wolff that Jung had informed her that in talking about his life, the meaning of many things had now become clear to him.[61] The memoir was called "From the earliest

---

57. *Ibid.*

58. Jaffé to Alwina von Keller, 25 August 1959, JA (filed with Jung's correspondence to von Keller).

59. Jung to Jaffé, 27 October 1957, BA. Concerning the *Red Book*, only Jung's postscript to it was included as an appendix to the German edition of *Memories*. The *Red Book* could best be described as a literary work of psychology. In May 2000, the heirs of C. G. Jung decided to release the work for publication, so that it would be first made available to the public in a definitive scholarly edition, to be prepared by the present author.

60. 10 January 1958, BL.

61. *Ibid.*

experiences of my life", and was addressed to his children. It began
with the following lines:

> When I write, I always consciously or unconsciously have an audi-
> ence before me, and what I write is always a letter to the world, so
> I find you, my dear children, in the first row of my auditorium. I
> would like to inform you how I developed, that means to tell you
> the little which I can recall from the darkness of my youth.[62]

Jung informed Kurt Wolff that he was aware that this "collided in
a certain sense" with Jaffé's work, but thought that they could enter
into a collaboration.[63] Kurt Wolff was alarmed at the prospect of the
parallel publication of two Jung autobiographies, and went to
Switzerland to resolve the situation.[64] It was decided to include
Jung's memoir in the text of *Memories*. However, Jung wanted this
to be signed in his name and clearly demarcated from the rest of the
book. As Jaffé wrote to Kurt Wolff, "This caesura in the middle of
the book is important for him as an indication of the real situation."[65]

Jung's attitude towards the project fluctuated. On 14 October
1958, Jaffé wrote to Helen Wolff informing her that Jung wanted the
form of the work to change. He had only read the chapter on the
"confrontation with the unconscious". He was disturbed by the fact
that she had put different statements from different protocols on the
same theme together in a whole chapter, that in so doing she had
had to introduce much of her own comments in the first person
singular, and that much of what he had said to her had been
remoulded. Consequently, he suggested that she add short sections
of her own, like Eckermann, including her reactions and dreams,
instead of the connecting sentences.[66]

---

62. Jung, "From the earliest experiences of my life", JA, p. 1. On 22 May
1960, Richard Hull wrote to Kurt Wolff indicating that he had suggested cutting
this, and commencing with the line, "When I was six months old", as this would
be "the proper fairytale beginning" (BL). The passage was deleted in the
published version.
63. 1 February 1958, BL.
64. Kurt Wolff to Aniela Jaffé, 9 November, 1958, BL.
65. 19 October 1958, BL.
66. At one stage, a plan was considered simply to publish the protocols as
they were, but it was thought that they would be insufficiently accessible to the

In August 1959, Jung wrote to Kurt Wolff from Bollingen:

The present somewhat difficult and delicate situation of the book
has arisen because Frau A. Jaffé has become overextended due to
the nature of the material. I never intended to write a biography of
myself, as I knew that it would be no easy thing, but still yet
perhaps an impossible undertaking, which I would never dare to
approach. If I had ever dreamt that I would have attempted to write
an autobiography, it would have to be written according to my
view, namely not in a mere two-dimensional way, but three-dimen-
sional, that means with the inclusion of the unconscious and the
shadow, which shows that an actual body has entered the beam of
phenomenal consciousness.[67]

He added that as a result of this, he had had to intervene more, so
the balance of the work shifted. To rectify this situation, he had now
asked Jaffé to insert herself back into the work, and to add her
remarks into the text, in footnotes and at the beginning and end of
chapters.

However, after Jaffé did this, Kurt Wolff regarded the results as
catastrophic, as they broke the continuity of Jung's statements and
destroyed the atmosphere. Kurt Wolff wanted these removed, or
else placed in footnotes or the introduction.[68] Kurt Wolff complained that he found it hard to contact Jung directly, particularly
as Jaffé opened all his letters, and was present when they met.[69] As
for Jung's suggestions in his August letter, Kurt Wolff felt that the
work could have been presented as a dialogue, if it had been
conceived in this way at the beginning (and then ideally with someone like Erich Neumann, instead of Aniela Jaffé), but that one
couldn't introduce another voice into a monologue.[70]

---

reader. (Memo, Wolfgang Sauerlander to Helen Wolff, 18 October 1958, copy,
BP). On 29 January 1958, Jaffé wrote to Kurt Wolff that Jung had suggested
several times that she should publish the protocols and he would publish his
notes, but she did not think that this was seriously meant (BL).
    67. BL.
    68. Kurt Wolff to Cary Baynes, 18 September 1959, BP. He considered the
combination of the "I" form with the "he" form to be unworkable (Kurt Wolff
to Cary Baynes, 20 September, 1959, BL).
    69. Ibid.
    70. Ibid.

In February 1960, Jaffé informed Hull that Jung wanted to see him at the end of the month. Hull narrated:

> The old man turned up . . . said he wanted to talk, and talked solidly for over an hour about the autobiography. I gathered that there was some controversy going on as to the "authentic" text. (At this time I had seen no text at all.) He impressed upon me, with the utmost emphasis, that he had said what he wanted to say in his own way—"a bit blunt and crude sometimes"—and that he did not want his work to be "tantifiziert" ("auntified" or "oldmaidified", in Jack's felicitous phrase). "You will see what I mean when you get the text", he said. As he spoke at some length about the practice of "ghost-writing" by American publishers, I inferred that the "Tantifierung" would be done by Kurt. I thereupon asked Jung whether I would have the authority to "de-old maidify" the text supplied to me by Kurt. "In those cases", he said, "the big guns will go into action", pointing to himself. I found all this rather puzzling, because Kurt had said earlier that, especially in the first three chapters, the impact lay precisely in the highly personal tone and unorthodox outspokenness, which should at all costs be preserved.[71]

On 9 May 1960, Hull wrote to Kurt Wolff after reading a manuscript of the text with changes marked in green ink. He found that these changes toned down the vividness of Jung's expressions and commented that Jung's comments had initially led him to believe that Kurt Wolff was responsible for toning down the manuscript. Now, however, his suspicions were that it was Jaffé who was responsible for them. Hull had initially thought that Jung was merely unhappy about the connecting comments that Jaffé had added, and he noted that Jung had said to him, "She has written a lot of stuff about me which simply won't do." Hull now thought that she had been responsible for bowdlerizing the text. Subsequently, he came to think that Jung did not have her in mind, but his own family.[72]

---

71. Hull, "A record of events", BA, pp. 1–2.
72. Interview with Gene Nameche, CLM, p. 17. To this comment, Nameche added the following note: "Some persons believe it was Frau Jaffé as well as the family who wanted to 'auntify' Jung."

The question of who precisely Jung had in mind is of lesser insignificance than the consequences of the manner in which the text was assembled and edited. Two strata of alterations need to be distinguished. The first stratum consists in the manner in which Jaffé utilized materials from her interviews with Jung, and edited the manuscripts of Jung that she utilized.[73] The second stratum consists in changes made between the first manuscript she prepared and the published version. Many people were involved in the second stratum of changes. A number of alterations of the manuscript were made at the request of a representative of the Jung family at a late stage of the editorial process. A line by line comparison of the protocols with subsequent manuscripts and the published English and German versions, together with the study of editorial correspondences, shows that the bulk of the deletions and changes lie in the first stratum, ie., between the protocols, Jung's manuscripts, and the first German manuscript. While statements in the protocols that appear in the published version are generally reliably reproduced, in many cases the context, mood, and associative connections are lost. Whole sequences are remade with elements drawn from different sources in a form of mosaic work. This reordering often recasts the meaning of statements. In places, sentences spoken by Jung in various contexts and months apart were joined together to form a sequence of paragraphs. From a historical perspective, the protocols are far more important than the published versions.

Hull subsequently wondered whether the tension between Kurt Wolff's desire to publish Jung's autobiography and Aniela Jaffé's attempt to take over Lucy Heyer's project to write a biography was responsible for some of the difficulties which ensued.[74]

In her introduction, Jaffé claims that Jung "read through the manuscript of the book and approved it."[75] However, this simply could not have been the case, as Jung never saw the final manuscript. On 6 May 1961, one month before he died, Jung wrote to Gerald

---

73. When he made the comments above, Hull had not consulted the protocols.

74. Hull to Read, 2 September 1960, Routledge archives, University of Reading (hereafter, RA).

75. Jung/Jaffé, 1963, p. 9.

Gross, an editor at Pantheon, concerning his "biography". He expressed his regret at not being able to reread the chapters which he had "controlled" and asked him to send those which he hadn't controlled, "('Bollingen,' 'Visions, 'Life after Death' etc.)." He finished by saying that in the event of his incapacity, he entrusted Jaffé with the responsibility for final version of the manuscript.[76]

Memories was supposed to include a chapter entitled 'Encounters' ('Begegnungen'). There is an undated, late handwritten letter from Jung to Jaffé, in which he asked her what had happened to this. He noted that he had seen and partially spoken about, among others, Theodore Roosevelt, Paul Valéry, Rabbi Beck, Hitler, Mussolini, Goebbels, Miguel Serrano, Scheler, Toynbee, Eddington, Sir James Jeans, the Grossherzog of Hessen, Kaiser Wilhelm and Prince Heinrich, and Frobenius, and noted that "it is not 'encountered' ('begegnet')".[77] There is no written reply to this letter.

The manuscripts which Jung saw went through considerable editing after his death. An example of this is the following statement from the minutes of a discussion between Aniela Jaffé, Herr Rascher, and Fraulein Poggensee on 22 January 1962:

> Collins have made a few very good suggestions for abridgements, that she has followed. Above all, the "extraverted" and somewhat superficial accounts of London and Paris should be omitted, Africa somewhat cut, whilst all "introverted" sections should be extended and somewhat built up in places. The section of the meeting with James and Flornoy [sic] should further be cut according to Pantheon as well as those with Oeri and Zimmer, whereas we will retain these.[78]

It is critical to note that these deliberations concerning how introverted or extroverted the book should be, how many of Jung's travels should be included, and whether the likes of Flournoy, James, Oeri, and Zimmer were in or out took place after Jung's death. These are by no means minor changes (the chapters on Paris and London were among those that Jung had actually read through).[79]

---

76. JA.
77. JA. Jung discussed some of these figures in the protocols, Library of Congress (hereafter, LC).
78. RZ.
79. Jaffé to Wolff, 18 January 1961, BL.

The published version of *Memories* played an important role in fostering the Freudocentric legend of Jung's life and work. In *Memories*, the only section that is named after an individual is that on Freud, leaving the impression that the two most important figures in Jung's life were Freud and God, which has left commentators disputing which of these two comes first. This impression is strengthened in the American and English editions, as the appendices on Flournoy and Zimmer, which are in the German and French editions, are absent.[80] This strengthens the Freudocentric reading of Jung. The Countway manuscript presents a radically different organization. This version shows variant chapter arrangements that considerably alter the structure of the narrative. The section following the chapter on Freud is headed "Memories. Flournoy—James—Keyserling—Crichton Miller—Zimmer." This heading is then crossed out by hand, and replaced by "Théodore Flournoy and William James".[81] These variations alone show the contingency of the arrangement in *Memories*. Further, in this arrangement, the tributes to Flournoy and James directly follow the section on Freud.

In the chapter on Freud in *Memories*, Jung diagnoses Freud as suffering from a serious neurosis, and claims that his followers have not grasped the significance of their founder's neurosis.[82] For Jung, the universal claims made by Freud's psychology are invalid, due to Freud's neurosis. In the published version, the chapter that immediately follows portrays Jung's "confrontation with the unconscious" and his discovery of archetypes, and through the discovery of his own myth, a means for "modern man to find his soul". *Memories* furthers the myth of Jung's heroic descent and self-generation, after he has freed himself from the shackles of Freudian psychology, founding a foundling psychology, without antecedents, with no prior model to follow, only the counter exemplar of Freud.

The Countway manuscript presents a very different version. In the sections on Flournoy and James, which immediately follow the chapter on Freud, the problems as to how one could found a

---

80. Jung's tribute to Flournoy is published in English in Flournoy, 1994.
81. Countway ms., p. 197, CLM.
82. The chapter on Freud was drawn together from comments that Jung made at various moments during his interviews with Aniela Jaffé.

non-neurotic psychology, on which Jung claims Freud foundered, appear to be have already been answered in the affirmative before Freud, by Flournoy and James. Further, Jung portrays the positivity of the mentoring relation, through which no breaks were necessary. Jung credits their significance in helping him to formulate his criticisms of Freud, and furnish the methodological presuppositions for his formulation of a post-Freudian psychology.[83]

In the chapter on James, Jung gives an account of their contact, and attempts to spell out his intellectual debt to James. Jung recounts that he met James in 1909, and paid him a visit the following year. He said that James was one of the most outstanding persons that he ever met. He found him aristocratic, the image of a gentleman, yet free of airs and graces. He spoke to Jung without looking down on him, Jung felt that they had an excellent rapport. He felt that it was only with Flournoy and James that he could talk to easily, and that he revered his memory, and that he was a model for Jung. He found that both of them were receptive and of assistance with his doubts and difficulties, which he never found again. He esteemed James' openness and vision, which was particularly marked in his psychical research, which they discussed in detail, and his seances with the medium, Mrs Piper. He saw the far-reaching significance of psychical research as a means of access to the psychology of the unconscious. Jung said that he was also very influenced by James' work on the psychology of religion, which also became for him a model, in particular, the way in he managed to accept and let things stand, without forcing them into a theoretical bias.

There are also instances where Jung's specific recommendations were not carried out. The significance of Jung's relation to Richard Wilhelm is indicated by the fact that Jung wanted the text that Richard Wilhelm had written about him in 1929, "My Encounter with C. G. Jung in China", included as an appendix.[84] Jung was also

---

83.   For Jung's relation to James, see Taylor, 1980, and Shamdasani, 2003.

84.   *Neue Zürcher Zeitung*, 21 January 1929. Jaffé to Wolff, 19 December, 1960, BL. In the Countway manuscript, a four page excerpt from this was included in the text as an appendix (CLM, pp. 523–526). In his tribute, Wilhelm noted that Jung's insights parallelled those of the Far East, and he pointed out the close similarities. He noted that it was much harder for a Westerner like

sceptical about the prologue to the book, finding its style "too femi-
nine" and "aesthetic".[85]

A number of the chapters in the book are based on Jung's own
writings. Here again, the manuscripts Jung wrote do not exactly
correspond to what was printed in the final work. One sees this
clearly in her treatment of Jung's "From the earliest experiences of
my life." Some passages were deleted, and other passages were
added by Jaffé from her interviews, and further changes were made
by others involved in the project.[86]

Selectivity is an inherent part of any editorial process, and it is
quite legitimate for a biographer to shape their materials according
to their own perspectives. Critical problems enter, however, when a
particular biographer's account is identified with a subject's own
self-understanding. In my view, this is precisely what occurred in
the case of *Memories, Dreams, Reflections*, and has been the cause of
endless misunderstandings.

Jung to reach them, which is perhaps why he hadn't been appreciated in
Europe. Wilhelm thought that it was not by chance that when he returned from
China with ancient Chinese wisdom, he found that he could discuss these
matters with Jung, to whom he owed many suggestions. He suggested that
there were three possible explanations for the remarkable parallels between
Jung's ideas and those of the ancient Chinese sages: first, that Jung had been
Chinese in a past life; second, that Jung was telepathic; and third, which was the
explanation that Wilhelm accepted, that the Chinese sages and Jung both
descended to the depths of the collective psyche where they encountered the
same states of being, and their agreement demonstrated the essential truth of
their conceptions.

85.   Jaffé to Wolff, 19 October, 1958, BL.

86.   Countway ms., CLM; Hull draft translation, LC; Draft translation, BL.
During the editing, there was some discussion about one passage in the manuscript. In Hull's draft translation of Jung's boyhood fantasy concerning Basle
Cathedral, the manuscript reads: "God sits on his golden throne, high above the
world, and ~~shits on the cathedral~~; from under the throne ~~falls~~ an enormous turd
falls" (p. 32, LC). In the Countway manuscript, the same passage reads: "God
sits on his golden throne, high above the world, and ~~shits on the cathedral~~ [in
hand: shits on his church]" (CLM, p. 32). Bair commented that neither Jaffé nor
Marianne Niehus would permit Jung to use the word "shit" in this context,
suggesting that it was censored (2003, p. 635). However, the original German
typescript reads: "unter dem Thron fällt ein ungeheures Excrement" ("an enormous excrement falls under the throne") (JA, p. 19). This manuscript is on open
access. This correctly reproduces Jung's handwritten manuscript (Jung family
archives, personal communication, Ulrich Hoerni).

In this regard, the status of *Memories* is quite critical. Rather than being seen as one biography among others, it was seen as Jung's autobiography. Hull highlighted the significance of this issue:

> there is all the difference in the world between a book advertised as "The Autobiography of C.G. Jung" and a book of Jung's memoirs edited by Aniela Jaffé (of whom few have heard). One is an automatic bestseller, the other is not.[87]

In the notes of a meeting with Aniela Jaffé on 15 November 1959, Helen Wolff noted that Jaffé thought that people wanted to separate her from the book to have it as only Jung's book, so as to make it a bestseller. Consequently, Helen Wolff noted that it had to be left to Jung to decide in which form the autobiography should appear, and whether it should appear as an autobiography.[88]

Given their rights to Jung's own writings, it was natural to expect that Jung's existing German and English publishers would have liked to publish the work. Furthermore, Jung's increasing involvement in the text brought this issue to the foreground, and it was taken up both by Rascher Verlag and Routledge. In the minutes of a meeting between Dr Karrer and Mr Niehus (representing Jung) and Mr Rascher and Mrs Poggensee on 23 March 1959, it is noted:

> Dr. Karrer reported that a few years ago Pantheon Books (Dr. Wolff) proposed to Mrs. Jaffé to write a biography of Jung, possibly in the form of conversations with Jung . . . But now the matter has developed differently than was previously planned, in that Prof. Jung has become more and more drawn in, so that from an "object of observation" he has become a co-worker.[89]

For Rascher, this raised the question of whether the work would fall under the existing contracts. After a further meeting a few months later, it is noted in the minutes that "One still does not know, if the book will sail under the flag 'Jung' or 'Jaffé'".[90]

---

87. Hull, "A record of events", p. 4, BA.
88. BL.
89. RZ.
90. "Aktennotiz über Besprechung zwischen Herrn Dr. Karrer, Herrn Niehus, Herrn Rascher, sr., Herr Albert Rascher und Fr. Poggensee, 1 May 1959. It is also noted in the minutes that "Herr Niehus added that Herr Prof. Jung himself did not want the word 'autobiography' to be used." RZ.

Similar questions were raised by Routledge and Kegan Paul. In a letter of 18 December 1959, Cecil Franklin wrote to Jung:

> I believe that the history of this book is that it started as a work by Aniela Jaffé which she would have written with your close help; but that it grew out of that and far beyond it until it became in fact your autobiography . . . We have looked into our agreement for 1947 and find that if this is indeed your autobiography . . . publishing rights would be with us . . . We have looked forward to the time when we might publish your autobiography . . . It would worry us very much and might harm our reputation over here to be considered the publishers only of your more strictly technical books.[91]

Did Jung regard the work as his autobiography? During the composition of the work it was variously referred to by those involved as the "biography", the "Vita", the "autobiography", the "so-called biography", and the "so-called autobiography", including by Jung himself.[92] On 5 April 1960, Jung wrote to Walter Niehus-Jung, his son-in-law and literary executor:

> I want to thank you for your efforts on behalf of my so-called "Autobiography" and to confirm once more that I do not regard this book as my undertaking but expressly as a book which Frau A. Jaffé has written... The book should be published under her name and not under mine, since it does not represent an autobiography composed by myself.[93]

On 25 May 1960, Herbert Read wrote to John Barrett concerning the book:

> It now appears it will have some such title as:

---

91.   19 December 1959, BA.
92.   According to Hull, Jung at one time suggested that the work could be titled, "Fragments from an Unintentional Autobiography." (Hull to Kurt Wolff, 2 June 1960, BL).
93.   Adler, 1975, p. 550, tr. mod. Bair described this letter as 'curious' and claimed that it indicated power which Marianne and Walther Niehus had (2003, p. 606–607). However, as the documents cited here show, this letter is in consonance with a number of other critical statements by Jung.

Aniela Jaffé

"Reminiscences, Dreams, Thoughts"

with contributions from C.G. Jung.[94]

Following these negotiations, a resolution of the Editorial Committee of the *Collected Works* of Jung was drawn up, allowing the book to be published outside of the exclusive contracts with the Bollingen Foundation and Routledge and Kegan Paul. It contains the following statement:

> C. G. Jung has always maintained that he did not consider this book as his own enterprise but expressly as a book written by Mrs. Jaffé. The chapters written by C. G. Jung were to be considered as his contributions to the work of Mrs. Jaffé. The book was to be published in the name of Mrs. Jaffé and not in the name of C. G. Jung, because it did not represent an autobiography composed by C. G. Jung (letter of C. G. Jung to Walter Niehus dated 5th April 1960).

> On a conference held on the 26th August between Prof. C. G. Jung, Mr. John Barrett, Miss Vaun Gillmor, Sir Herbert Read, Mr. and Mrs. W. Niehus-Jung and Mrs. Aniela Jaffé, C. G. Jung confirmed again that he did strictly consider this book as an undertaking of Mrs. A. Jaffé to which he had only given his contributions... The Editorial Committee decides hereby formally that it will not approve any decision of the Executive Subcommittee which would add the book of Mrs. A. Jaffé to the Collected Works.[95]

These statements are quite emphatic and unambiguous. However, in Helen and Kurt Wolff's view, these formulations were

---

94. BA.
95. "Resolution of the Editorial Committee for 'The Collected Works' of Prof. C. G. Jung", BA. Signed by Jung on 29 November 1960, and by John Barrett on 13 December 1960. Vaun Gillmor of the Bollingen Foundation provided the following account of this meeting: "On the subject of the biography being prepared by Frau Jaffe, Dr. Jung stated that he wishes this book to be called a biography as told to Frau Jaffe. He also stated that he himself has written three chapters of the book, the remaining being written by Frau Jaffe from notes taken in conversation from him. He specifically stated that he does not wish the work to be considered as his as he has only contributed to the book of Frau Jaffe." "Conversation with Dr. Jung 26 August 1960", BA.

ruses to resolve the situation with Rascher and Routledge.[96] Helen Wolff wrote to Cary Baynes on 9 June 1960:

> You are quite right in saying that if the book appears under Aniela's name it is sure to be a dud—people are not interested in Aniela Jaffé, but in C. G. Jung. Besides, it really is *his* book, and in his heart he knows it is his. I wonder who gave him the idea that it is not good enough to be his.[97]

It is quite clear that Kurt Wolff's original intention was to publish Jung's autobiography, and that he was fully aware of the different sales potential of an autobiography and a biography of Jung. In my view, Jung's statements that the work should not be regarded as his autobiography are fully consistent with his previous statements spelling out why he did not want to undertake an autobiography, and the nature of his collaboration with Jaffé. On 6 January 1960, he wrote to Emma von Pelet:

> I have always vowed to myself that I would never write an autobiography and in this case I have only wetted my feet a little; it is rather Frau Jaffé who is writing a biography of me to which I have made a few contributions.[98]

In that year, Pantheon was bought by Random House, and Kurt and Helen Wolff took no further part in the project. In 1961, Jung died on 6 June. Obituaries appeared prominently in newspapers and periodicals around the world. The following year, extracts from *Memories* appeared in *Die Weltwoche* and *Atlantic Monthly*. The first extract in *Die Weltwoche* was simply titled "The autobiography of C. G. Jung". The book itself appeared in 1962 in English and German. A French edition appeared in 1966, entitled, *My Life: Memories, dreams and thoughts*.[99]

---

96. Helen Wolff to Cary Baynes 13 July 1960, BP.
97. BP.
98. Adler, 1975, p. 531, tr. mod.
99. "Die Autobiographie von C. G. Jung", *Die Weltwoche*, 31 August, 1962. Other items in the German edition that were missing in the English editions were a letter by Jung to a "young student", Jung's postscript to his *Red Book* and "Details about C. G. Jung's family" by Aniela Jaffé. The latter item was published in English in *Spring*, 1984. There are many discrepancies between the

What was indeed a remarkable biography has been mistakenly read as an autobiography.[100] The widely held assumption that the work was Jung's 'autobiography', together with the first person narrative gave the work a definitive status in all literature on Jung for the next three decades, which it otherwise would never have possessed.[101]

In 1980, Jaffé signed a contract with Bonz Verlag for a book entitled *Erlebtes und Gedachtes*, which drew further material from the remaining protocols, including a chapter on Toni Wolff.[102] Jaffé had been advised that she had the rights to the material and had not asked the Jung heirs for permission, and a lawsuit ensued.[103] The work remains unpublished and complex issue of the rights to the protocols awaits resolution.

German and English editions, notably numerous passages in the former that are missing from the latter. Some, but by no means all, were published in English by Shoji Muramoto (1987).

100.   In response to my first paper on this subject, the late Franz Jung wrote to me: "It gives me at least some proofs, what I before only guessed, that not everything has run straight and we do not even know in what extent C. G. J. was aware of and agreed to the formulation or the omissions Frau Jaffé, Hull or even third parties were actually doing. /It is very good that you recalled to our memories the letter April 5th 1960 and the letter of Herbert Read to J. Barrett, 25th May 1960, with proposing a title which makes clear who the author was. To day most people do not know these statements and take wrong conclusions." (14 August 1995, personal possession.)

101.   In the late 1980s, research on the composition of the text was concurrently and independently undertaken by Alan Elms and myself (see Elms 1994 and Shamdasani 1995). Prior to this, the status of the text was unquestioned in the public domain. Bair claimed that the divergences between the English and German editions caused led to speculation concerning censorship between scholars from the moment that the work was published (2003, p. 638). This was simply not the case, as there was no public debate concerning censorship until our research was published. In her footnote, she wrote: "most prominent among them Shamdasani and Elms, who base many of their charges on incomplete evidence and non-objective speculation" (p. 847, n. 69). No evidence is given of this, and Bair does not even provide the reference for anything that I have written on the subject.

102.   Jung discussed his relationship with Toni Wolff in the protocols, LC, p. 98, pp. 171–174; see Shamdasani, 1995, pp. 124–125. Bair stated that in the protocols she read, there was no discussion of this (2003, p. 838, n. 61).

103.   Gerda Niedieck to William McGuire, 20 January 1981, McGuire papers, LC.

"Cheated by the Master"

Memories was not the only authorized biographical study of Jung that appeared at this time. Shortly after Jung's death, a work on Jung appeared by his friend, the English psychiatrist, E. A. Bennet. In his introduction, Bennet noted that the plan of the book had been discussed with Jung, and as Jung had read the work in typescript and annotated it, it could fairly be taken that "the statements made here are in accordance with his views".[104] Thus, the book was billed as an authorized study of Jung, written with his co-operation.

Bennet stated that the initial plan had been for him to write a biography of Jung, and added that to this end, Jung had provided a great deal of information about his life. However, Bennet noted,

> on reflection he thought this would be an almost impossible undertaking because of the variety of his work and the complexity of his personality. In the end he decided that he must write an autobiography, and he has done so (a part of a volume—a *Life*—since written by Mrs. Aniela Jaffé). He finished this far from congenial task—as he described it—in September 1959.[105]

Bennet does not refer to Aniela Jaffé's work as constituting Jung's autobiography, rather as incorporating it, by which he had in mind the first three chapters, "From the earliest experiences of my life".

Some of Bennet's conversations with Jung that he recorded were subsequently published by his wife. In one conversation, on 30 August 1956, Jung spoke of the difficulties involved in writing his biography:

> At breakfast C. G. spoke of the difficulties implicit in the idea of anyone writing his biography; he said it would require a full understanding of his thought, and no one understood it completely. Freud's life, he said, could be easily described because his thought was simply laid out. But with him it was more complex, for unless the development of his thought were central to his biography it would be no more than a series of incidents, like writing the biography of Kant without knowing his work.[106]

---

104. Bennet, 1961, p. viii.
105. *Ibid.*, p. vii.
106. Bennet, 1982, p. 61.

Jung's comments here are significant, in terms of the way that *Memories* has been subsequently understood. For many, the biographical details it contained have been taken as the key to the understanding of Jung's work, which is diametrically opposite to the position that Jung puts forward here.

Jung's comments here can be regarded as an elaboration of his oft-repeated comments concerning the significance of the personal equation for understanding a particular psychology: that it is necessary to grasp the psychologist's *psychology* to understand their life.

As illustration of this point, Jung narrated to Bennet a "momentous" dream that he had in 1913 during his "confrontation with the unconscious", which was a big turning point in his life, and commented that if it were related, few people would understand the significance it had at that point in his career. The dream was as follows:

> He was climbing a steep mountain path, twisting to the top, and on the right the valley was in shadow for it was still night; ahead the sun was behind the peak and rising, but still hidden. In front of him was a primitive man (the man of all ages—brown-skinned and hairy); he was following this man and each was armed for hunting, probably chamois. Then the sun rose, and on the summit of the mountain Siegfried appeared in shining armour with a shield and spear; he was wearing something like skis and glided down over the rocks. The skis were of bones—the bones of the dead. Then the primitive man indicated to him that they must shoot Siegfried with their rifles, and they lay in wait for him and killed him. The primitive man (the shadow) was the leader; he went to collect the spoil. But C. G. was filled with remorse and rushed down the mountain into a ravine and up the other side—he had to get away from the awful crime. It was raining and everything was wet; but while this washed away all traces of the crime it made no difference to the sense of guilt which oppressed his conscience.[107]

Bennet went on to note Jung's reactions to the dream:

> He awoke and wanted to sleep again but he knew he must try to understand the dream. For a while his remorse for murdering Siegfried—the hero—obliterated everything else, overwhelming him to the extent that he felt impelled to take his revolver from the drawer and shoot himself,

---

107.   *Ibid.*, pp. 61–62.

"commit suicide"; the dream and the impulse were terribly vivid and he might have done it but for the fact that his thoughts about the dream were beginning to take shape: the hero, doing the very heroic act, was killed by the primitive man. That is, the dream was pointing to the primitive man, who was immoral or undeveloped in our eyes, as the leader, the one to be followed. For him, this meant that he must follow not the here and now of consciousness, the accepted achievements, but the man of the ages who represented the collective unconscious, the archetypes.[108]

As we shall see from the comments which subsequent biographers have made on this dream, there is something prophetic in Jung's citation of it to indicate how easily the crucial turning points in his life could be misconstrued.

On 5 September 1956, Bennet wrote to Jung indicating that Ruth Bailey had suggested that he write a biography of Jung. On 10 October, Jung wrote to him:

As you know, I am a somewhat complicated phenomenon, which hardly can be covered by one biographer only . . . Therefore I should like to make you a similar proposition, namely that you proceed along your line as a medical man like Philp has done on his part as a theologian. Being a doctor you would inquire into the anamnesis of your patient and you would ask the questions and I would answer as a patient would answer. Thus you would move along the lines of your habitual thinking and would be enabled to produce a picture of my personality understandable at least to more or less medical people. Philp certainly would produce a picture of my religious aspect, equally satisfactory. Since it is undeniable that one of several aspects is medical, another theological, a biography written by specialists in their field has the best chance of being accurate, although not comprehensive in as much as the specific psychological synthesis would demand somebody equally at home in

---

108. *Ibid.*, p. 62. In 1925, Jung had said of this dream: "The hero . . . is the symbol of the greatest value recognized by us . . . it appeared as if Siegfried were my hero. I felt an enormous pity for him, as though I myself had been shot. I must then have had a hero I did not appreciate, and it was my ideal of force and efficiency I had killed. I had killed my intellect, helped on to the deed by a personification of the collective unconscious, the little brown man with me. In other words, I deposed my superior function" (Jung, 1925, p. 57).

primitive psychology, mythology, history, parapsychology and science—and even in the field of artistic experience.[109]

Thus, as Jung saw it, any biography of him would inevitably be shaped by the presuppositions and personal equation of the biographer. The multi-faceted nature of his life and work meant that there simply couldn't be a definitive biography of him.

Bennet accepted Jung's suggestion, and sent him a list of questions.[110] Jung replied that would be too long to give written answers, so he invited Bennet over for a fortnight.[111] He added the following reflections on the undertaking:

> The whole thing is a ticklish task and it seems to be rather difficult because the average reader would hardly be capable of understanding what it is all about. I have been exposed to so many misunderstandings that I am rather scared to tell the truth about my biography, as I see it. I should therefore prefer, you should first try to find your way through the jungle of memories.[112]

It is possible that it was precisely because Jung thought that there was no single individual with sufficient grasp of his psychology to write his biography, that he deliberately narrated some of the same material to Bennet as to Jaffé, so that neither would be the only account. On 11 January 1957, Aniela Jaffé informed Kurt Wolff that Jung was of the view that her work and Bennet's would not overlap, as they were completely different people and would have different viewpoints. Thus, questions like Jung's relation to Freud and Charcot would probably be dealt with by Bennet.[113]

On 14 January, Bennet wrote to Jung, "Your commendation of the plan that I should write a biography, based on your contributions to medicine, was most cheering."[114]

---

109. JA, original in English. Howard Philp had also been considering a biographical work on Jung. After modifications, the outcome of Philp's was his *Jung and the Problem of Evil* (1959). Jung's replies to his questions were also reproduced in *CW* 18 under the title "Jung and religious belief".

110. Bennet to Jung, 7 December 1956, JA.

111. Jung to Bennet, 10 December 1956, JA, orig. in English.

112. *Ibid.*

113. BL.

114. JA.

This issue of the relation of Bennet's project to Jaffé's project is further taken up in a conversation that Bennet noted with Jung's daughter, Marianne Niehus, on 24 March 1959:

> I told her C.G. had already written much of his autobiography (I remember him talking of the difficulties of writing about his life a year or two ago and perhaps this put the idea into his mind). She said Mrs. Jaffé wanted to publish what he had written. I gave her my Introduction to read. She said my approach was quite different from Mrs. Jaffé's and pressed me to continue. She said that mine was more masculine, and the fact that another biography was in preparation should not prevent me from going on with it.[115]

Thus, Marianne Niehus seemed to regard both projects as authorized biographies of a roughly similar status.

On 7 February 1959, Jung wrote to Bennet,

> Concerning your plan to write something about the "development of my ideas and their impact on medicine", it pleases me very much. There are, of course, no objections from my part against your incorporating some of our early talks in the books.[116]

While Jung was seemingly unconcerned with the overlap between Bennet's project and Jaffé's, she was of another opinion. On 20 July 1961, Kurt Wolff wrote to Cary Baynes, conveying Jaffé's reaction to reading Bennet's book:

> Aniela has fits about the book and I well understand why: Jung told Bennet not all but quite a lot of the stuff he dictated Aniela for the autobiography—many of his dreams for instance, among them the Basler Münster dream—and now his book comes out before the autobiography will be published in Spring. Aniela feels cheated by the Master.[117]

From this, it appears that Jaffé was initially unaware that Jung was telling Bennet some of the same personal material that he was

---

115. Bennet 1982, p. 111.
116. JA. Original in English.
117. BP.

telling her, which she had thought was on an exclusive basis. While there was little that one could do about Bennet's book, as it had already appeared, it was still possible to delay the publication of a German edition. On 9 March 1962, Rascher wrote to Gerald Gross, the editor for the book at Pantheon:

> There is hardly a day without enquiries from booksellers and private readers concerning the book, and much worse, of news of publishers and privates announcing biographies of C. G. Jung's to be in preparation—some of them based on personal informative material of Prof. Jung himself. In order to avoid that the most important of them, written by Dr. Bennet, might come out before the above memoirs, we have acquired the rights for the German edition, trying to wait with bringing this out, so that the Jung–Jaffé memoirs might be first.[118]

To delay a book's appearance is one of the more unusual reasons for acquiring the rights to it.

However, despite the overlap, Jaffé need not have feared. While *Memories* went on to be a bestseller, and regarded as the single most significant source on Jung's life, Bennet's book has all but disappeared. Long out of print, it is a work that is rarely cited, and which has been all but forgotten, despite the significant information it contains, such as a detailed correspondence between Jung and Bennet on the nature of scientific proof and psychology.[119]

Bennet's book was published in London by Barrie & Rockliff. Judging by the scarcity of reviews, their publicity budget was nothing like that of Random House or Collins. Indeed, Bennet's book does not seem to have even been mentioned in the copious reviews of *Memories*, which all gave the impression that the latter provided the first glimpse of Jung's intimate life.

Bennet himself wrote a review of *Memories* in the *British Medical Journal*, entitled "Jung's inner life". His review consisted of a sympathetic portrait of Jung, and only his opening paragraph directly addressed *Memories*, where he stated: "It is an unusual book and

118.   RZ.
119.   Bennet's subsequent study, *What Jung Really Said* (1966), has been far more successful, despite containing less historical material directly from Jung.

apparently it has been a great problem to reviewers, many of whom accepted it as an autobiography. Certainly it is not that."[120] Bennet was almost alone amongst commentators to state this point.

While there are interesting discrepancies between the details of some of Jung's memories and dreams in Bennet's and Jaffé's book, by far the most important is the fact that the latter is written in the first person. Had it not been for this, the subsequent fates of these two books might not have been so radically different. In 1982, Bennet's widow, Eveline Bennet, published a selection from his diaries detailing his conversations with Jung. Ironically, it is this work that most resembles one of the prototypes of *Memories*, Eckermann's *Conversations with Goethe*.

---

120.   23 September, 1963.

CHAPTER TWO

The incomplete works of Jung

Alongside attempts to write Jung's biography, endeavours were under way to publish his works. The fate of this project was to have critical and unsuspected consequences for subsequent biographies, and indeed, for all studies of Jung. For the volumes which have been produced: *The Collected Works*, several volumes of seminars and correspondences, leave much to be desired, and are glaringly incomplete. Thus, the biographies of Jung which have been written, together with the secondary literature, have based themselves on a textual corpus which is not altogether solid.

When first presented by Jack Barrett of the Bollingen Foundation with a copy of the first volume of the *Collected Works* to be published, Jung complained that it looked like a coffin.[121] The project of a collected edition of Jung's writings was proposed by Herbert Read, who was at that time an editorial director at Kegan Paul in 1945 (Kegan Paul became Routledge & Kegan Paul in 1947).

---

121. Personal communication, Ximena Roelli. To Richard Hull, Jung wrote that he far preferred the jacket and binding of Routledge's edition to the "coffin-like appearance" of the Bollingen edition (Jung to Hull, 6 July, 1953, LC).

At the same time, the Bollingen Foundation in America put forward a similar proposal. An agreement was reached in 1947 to jointly publish the works. At Jung's suggestion, Michael Fordham was appointed as the editor.[122] As Fordham was not fluent in German, Jung suggested that Gerhard Adler be appointed to check the translations. Jung considered it absolutely necessary to have this done by a native German-speaker.[123] For Jung, the manner in which he used language was an integral part of his psychology. On 17 June 1952, he wrote to Zvi Werblowsky,

> the language I speak must be equivocal, that is *ambiguous*, to do justice to psychic nature with its double aspect. I strive consciously and deliberately for ambiguous expressions, because it is superior to unequivocalness and corresponds to the nature of being.[124]

Jung commented to Fordham on the special problems confronting any translator of his works:

> my German style is by no means simple and it wants a specifically trained ear to hear the somewhat subtle innuendos which abound in certain articles . . . I find time and again that certain points are misunderstood or rendered badly by translators who do not grasp the full value of certain words . . . I'm rather anxious to have my works presented to the English public in an English form that

---

122.   In 1933, Fordham had gone to Zurich to meet Jung for training, and was turned down, due to the difficulty of foreigners finding work. (Fordham 1993, pp. 67–69). The date of this trip is confirmed by Fordham's diary (private possession, Max Fordham). Bair misdated this meeting to the early years of the Second World War and claimed that by this time Fordham was angry that Baynes had published an account of his analysis which was too easily recognizable (2003, p. 472). Baynes' *Mythology of the Soul* only appeared in 1940. Bair also claimed that until his death, Fordham insisted that he did not resent Jung, and alleged that his "grudge" towards him was as great as that towards Baynes (*ibid.*). Over the course of many conversations I held with Fordham between 1988 and 1995, I did not notice any resentment expressed towards Baynes or Jung: his attitude towards them was one of admiration and gratitude.

123.   Jung to Read, June 4 1946, RA. As the work progressed, Adler tended to restrict his work to dealing with specific queries raised by Hull (personal communication, Michael Fordham). In fairness to Adler, in my own experience, I have found that checking translations can take as much time as translating.

124.   Adler, 1975, p. 71, tr. mod.

expresses what the German text says. It needs somebody of course, who has a wider reading than psychiatry or academical psychology, since my language is often more literary than merely "scientific". I also happen to use allusions or quotations from classical literature, which, to an English reader would be perfectly strange.[125]

As Jung later told Herbert Read, he took the question of the translation of his work very seriously, particularly as he had had some annoying experiences.[126] Adler was also supposed to establish the equivalents for the German terminology, while Fordham was supposed to review the translation with a view to its English style.[127]

Fordham agreed to Adler being appointed as a translations editor, but Adler wanted to be on an equal footing with him. Fordham informed Herbert Read that he had met with Adler, who had told him that he wanted to be co-editor for the sake of his personal prestige. Fordham felt that he was not suited to the task, and furthermore, had also had doubts about his competency to check the translations, due to the poor quality of his English.[128] Jung thought that Adler's proposal was not a good idea, and felt that there should be one editor. He tried to convince Adler of this, but was unsuccessful.[129]

Richard Hull was appointed as the translator. The first work which Hull was assigned to translate was Jung's *Psychology and Alchemy*. Hull was a professional translator, with little prior exposure

---

125. 18 April 1946, Contemporary Medical Archives, Wellcome Trust Library for the History and Understanding of Medicine, London (hereafter, CMAC), orig. in English.

126. Jung to Read, 4 March 1948, RA.

127. Jung to Read, October 8 1946, Jung to Adler, 12 September 1946, RA.

128. ". . . his English is by no means good—it is heavy, gets overweighted with words." Fordham to Read, 3 July 1946, RA. Read had suggested the appointment of a separate translations editor, in which case, as Fordham saw it, Adler would be the second translations editor.

129. Jung to Read, 17 July 1946, RA. Bair claimed that most of Jung's correspondence during the *Collected Works* project was with Hull (2003, p. 582). This is not the case, as Jung had extensive correspondences with Gerhard Adler, Michael Fordham and Herbert Read.

to Jung's work.[130] He specialized in literary and philosophical works, and also translated Rilke's letters in 1946, and works by Martin Buber and Martin Heidegger in 1949. He was a published poet, and some who knew him recalled him as an ardent rationalist.[131]

In the notes of a meeting between Jung, Herbert Read, and Jack Barrett in 1949, it is recorded that: "Professor Jung remarks that Mr. Hull seems to have difficulty in understanding some of his (Jung's) concepts (f.i. the Self)."[132] Jung suggested that Hull should continue to collaborate with Barbara Hannah on future translations. Replying to Herbert Read concerning this plan to involve Hannah as a translation consultant, Hull informed him that this was a wish which he had confessed to nobody, as he had at times had trouble understanding Jung's ideas, and had not received sufficient clarification of this from Adler and Fordham when he was translating *Psychology and Alchemy*.[133] In 1953, Jung reviewed Hull's translation of his essay on Synchronicity, and wrote him that: "You certainly understand how to transform the heavy German grammatical forms into liquid English."[134] Indeed, Hull's translations are so fluent at a literary level that they generally do not read like a translation. A week later, Jung wrote to Barrett about Hull's translation:

> I have partially controlled Hull's translation of "Synchronicity" and have seen that it is absolutely necessary that somebody who understands the arguments of the paper, as well as German, should go with a fine comb through the translation that has already been controlled by Miss Hannah, and I therefore would propose that the ultimate translation should be given to Dr. Adler.[135]

Two years later, Jung again commented upon Hull's translation of the text in a letter to Michael Fordham:

---

130.   In accepting Read's invitation to take on the translation editorship for Jung's works, Hull wrote to him on 14 June 1946 that the only two books of Jung which he knew well were *Modern Man in Search of a Soul*, and *The Integration of the Personality* (RA).

131.   Personal communication, Ximena Roelli.

132.   RA.

133.   1 September 1949, RA.

134.   6 July 1953, LC, orig. in English.

135.   13 July 1953, BA, orig. in English.

I am returning to you by this same mail the galley proofs of "Synchronicity". My corrections are in the text. Hull has the unfortunate tendency to invent different words for one and the same concept; that's making for confusion.[136]

None of the editors was a trained scholar, and furthermore, the magnitude of the undertaking was not immediately apparent. As time went on, Adler and Fordham withdrew into a more supervisory role (which alone generated a sizeable correspondence). The bulk of the editorial work was subsequently carried out by William McGuire, Richard Hull, and Alan Glover. In recognition of this, McGuire was appointed Executive Editor in 1967 (Fordham suggested that Hull should have been as well, as his involvement went much further than translation).[137] Indeed, Hull saw his role as involving the silent correction of Jung's texts. To Herbert Read, he wrote:

Does it make sense to you that Jung's texts should be followed so faithfully that oversights, obscurities or inconsistencies of exposition should be reproduced, or should not be corrected save at the cost of an editorial explanation? What else are editors for, if not to clarify and correct where necessary, without drawing attention to themselves?[138]

---

136.   11 May 1955, CMAC, orig. in English. Bair claimed that Jung praised Hull's translations in all extant statements, and that there is no evidence that he had any reservations about them (2003, p. 583). The citations here indicate that this was not the case. In Hannah's view, as a "thinking type", Hull's translations left out feeling and the irrational. (1976, p. 334). Von Franz noted that Jung's writings had a double aspect, a logically understandable argument on the one hand, and on the other, the "unconscious" was allowed its say: "the reader . . . finds himself at the same time exposed to the impact of that 'other voice', the unconscious, which may either grip or frighten him off. That 'other voice' can, among other factors, be heard in Jung's special way of reviving the original etymological meanings of words and allowing both feeling and imaginative elements to enter into his scientific exposition." She noted that "unfortunately, this double aspect of Jung's writings has not been preserved in the monumental English edition of his Collected Works, translated by R. F. C. Hull" (Von Franz, 1972, p. 4). Franz Jung recalled heated discussions between Jung and Hull on issues of translation. He noted that Hull would come to see Jung with a completed translation, and would be unwilling to correct what he had done (personal communication).
137.   3 March 1967, CMAC. Fordham added that McGuire's role should be distinguished from theirs, as he did not have responsibility for major decisions.
138.   23 November 1964, RA. On one attempted major revision by Hull, see Shamdasani, 1994.

Those responsible for the *Collected Works* managed to make the bulk of Jung's published writings available in a comparatively short span of time from Jung's death. The value of this need not be stated. It has had an inestimable effect upon disseminating Jung's work and in fostering the development of the profession of analytical psychology in the English-speaking world. It is not incidental that the English-speaking world is where Jung's work has had its greatest impact. Furthermore, in their research in preparing the edition, the editors made many important contributions towards understanding the historical development of Jung's work. With the benefit of hindsight, numerous shortcomings are apparent. The manner in which these shortcomings have hindered the comprehension of Jung's work, as well as that of its development, needs to be pointed out. These hindrances remain hindrances only so long as individuals rely unquestioningly upon the *Collected Works*, and regard the task of the editing of Jung's work as one which has already been completed.

The first major difficulties with the *Collected Works* is its choice of its contents. At Jung's request, the plan for the German edition of his works, edited by Marianne Niehus-Jung, Lena Hurwitz Eisner, Franz Riklin Jr, Lilly Jung-Merker, Elisabeth Rüf, and Leonie Zander, followed that of the English edition.[139] This was carried out. Consequently, decisions made concerning the editing of the English edition were also carried over into the German edition. So many of the problems with the English edition apply equally to the German edition. However, there was insufficient co-ordination between the two editions, and the editors of the German edition seem not to have been aware of revisions that Jung specifically undertook for the English edition. Consequently, there are places where the English addition contains significant material not represented in the German edition.[140]

---

139. "Vorwort der Herausgeber" *GW* 16, p. 9. On the history of the German *Gesammelte Werke*, see Paul Bishop, 1998.

140. Hull wrote to Fordham that the Swiss editors were not fully aware of the changes which Jung made for the English edition (13 March 1969, CMAC). An example of this is Jung's paper on "synchronicity" (*CW* 8), where important passages written for the English edition were not carried back into the German edition.

A major difficulty that confronted the editors was that there was no complete bibliography of Jung's writings. New texts were continually emerging. Furthermore, after Jung's death, a great deal of further material came to light, in various stages of completion. This was referred to as the "floating material". The question of what to do with this material came to a head at a meeting held in Küsnacht in 1964 between Marianne Niehus, Walter Niehus, Franz Riklin, Aniela Jaffé, Herbert Read, John Barrett, and Vaun Gillmor. The question of the final disposition of the floating material centred on the desirability for a further volume of miscellaneous items, which was informally referred to as the "junk volume". Those present at the meeting came out against the need for such a volume, and also against the proposal that Hull be permitted to prepare a new translation of original 1912 edition of *Transformations and Symbols of the Libido*, which Jung had extensively rewritten in 1952. These discussions revealed that there were fundamental tensions as to what the *Collected Works* should be. As Herbert Read put it to Richard Hull,

> It is now quite clear that Fordham and Adler have always had a different conception of the Collected Works from any that I have entertained. My idea was an authorised version which would present a final authoritative text of what Jung wished preserved. It now appears that Fordham and Adler have been fighting all the time for what one can only call a variorum edition. They attach great importance to everything Jung ever wrote and argue that the Collected Works should present the development of his thought.[141]

Those present at the Küsnacht meeting came out strongly in favour of Read's conception (of those not present, Hull supported Read, and McGuire supported Adler and Fordham). Adler and Fordham felt that their authority was being undermined. The latter had undertaken the project in the understanding that *all* of Jung's published works were to be included, and, as he quite simply informed Read, "I have no criteria by which to exclude anything that Jung wrote".[142] In these discussions, both parties claimed that their proposals would have had the support of Jung.

---

141.   29 March 1962, RA.
142.   5 May 1964, RA.

While the "junk" volume finally went ahead, the selection of material that went into was heavily curtailed. The significance of this was that the full extent of Jung's literary remains was simply not known at the time of the Küsnacht meeting, and it wasn't until 1993 that a catalogue was prepared. The amount of unpublished material in this catalogue far exceeded what was previously known about.

As they stand, the Collected Works are far closer to Read's ideal than to Fordham and Adler's. As a consequence, while there is a Collected Works of Jung, this is far from being a Complete Works of Jung. Critically important published and unpublished writings by Jung remain outside the Collected Works. The former category contains items that were known about and excluded, as well as items which weren't. Thus, there are many papers by Jung that are as important as anything in the Collected Works that have remained unknown to this day.[143]

Despite the fact that Jung himself was in favour of a strictly chronological approach, the editors adopted a thematic arrangement.[144] Through the course of his career, Jung frequently revised his works and published different versions of essays in different contexts. Except for a few instances, the editors chose as a matter of policy to include what they took to be the final version of a particular work. However, what constituted a final version was not always clear. This has had the consequence that historically critical formulations and statements of Jung are simply not to be found in the Collected Works. One example of this is Jung's pivotal 1917 book, The Psychology of the Unconscious Processes.[145] Another example is a short but important paper published by Jung and Bleuler detailing their disagreements concerning the aetiology of dementia

---

143. A number of these are studied in Shamdasani, 2003.

144. Fordham to Jack Barrett, 2 Jan 1948, BA. As Fordham informed me, Jung took a laissez faire attitude to his editors, and generally left them to their own devices.

145. This book was a reworking and greatly expanded version of Jung's 1912 essay "New paths in psychology". The essay and the final version alone appear in the Collected Works. Realizing the importance of the 1917 edition, Hull had wanted to do a new translation of it, but was not given the go-ahead.

praecox.[146] Furthermore, a result of this approach is that one is often unable to ascertain when a particular passage was written, which makes it difficult, if not impossible, to study the development of his work on the basis of the *Collected Works*.[147]

The reproduction of Jung's works was not without errors, and certain passages in the original editions were not reproduced in the *Collected Works* edition. Thus, what is supposed to be the text of the first edition of "The structure of the unconscious" of 1916 does not exactly correspond to what was published in the *Archives de Psychologie*. Some of the editorial notes contain errors. A note in *CW* 18 states that Jung contributed abstracts in 1908 to *Folia neuro-biologica* and that "as these are summaries without critical comment, they are not translated but merely listed here."[148] However, if one inspects these abstracts, one sees that this is not actually the case. An editorial note states that a 1907 paper of Jung's "Associations d'idées familiales" was not included because its contents were similar to Jung's Clark University Lecture, "The family constellation" despite the fact that the former has several pages of important material not in the latter.[149]

The editorial apparatus to the *Collected Works*, while providing some important historical information, is minimal, and the edition is far from being a critical historical edition. The level of information provided in the editorial apparatus is far inferior to that present in *The Standard Edition* of Freud's work, let alone in critical historical editions like Harvard University Press's works of William James, or indeed the Bollingen Foundation's exemplary edition of the works of Samuel Taylor Coleridge. Thus, for example, information

---

146. As Fordham informed McGuire "Hull was against publishing the Bleuler/Jung discussion . . . I feel fairly sure Read would be against it, which leaves me in a minority of one . . ." (10 May, 1960, BA). Not incidentally, Fordham was the only person involved who had a background in psychiatry.

147. One author who dispensed completely with the *Collected Works* and relied on first editions was C. A. Meier, in his multi-volume text book, *The Psychology of C. G. Jung*. He indicated that only in such a manner was it possible to follow the original course of development of Jung's ideas, and to place them in context (1984, p. xii). It is not coincidental that this forms the most reliable exposition of Jung's work.

148. *CW* 18 § 1025.

149. *CW* 2, § 999.

from correspondences and manuscript drafts that sheds light on the composition of the books and essays in question is not noted, nor are sufficient notes added to contextualize and explain Jung's references.

The English translation, while stylistically fluent at a literary level, leaves a great deal to be desired, containing interpolations, reformulations, and misunderstood concepts and general errors. A full consideration of Hull's work is beyond the scope of this chapter. The following are some brief examples. In "Theoretical reflections on the essence of the psychical", a sentence occurs which states that the tragedy of psychology was that it had "no self-consistent mathematics at is disposal, but only a calculus of subjective prejudices".[150] The last clause is not found in the original German. In "On the archetypes of the collective unconscious", a sentence occurs in English which reads: "what comes after the door is, surprisingly enough, a boundless expanse of full of unprecedented uncertainty . . .".[151] Instead of a door (Tor), the word in German is death (Tod). Due to this error, the next few sentences are rendered meaningless. In "The relation of psychotherapy to the cure and of souls", a sentence occurs in English which reads, "the attitude of the psychotherapist is infinitely more important than the theories and methods of psychotherapy".[152] The last part of this sentence should be, "psychological theories and methods". The crux of the sentence lies in the contrast between psychotherapy and psychology. In Jung's inaugural address at the founding of the Jung Institute in Zürich in 1948, Jung stated that, "For psychotherapy, casuistic dream research in connection with comparative symbolism would be of great practical value".[153] This sentence is omitted altogether in the English translation. I concur with Paul Bishop's view that "Jung's reputation would grow to a large extent on a corrupt English version of his texts".[154] In my view and in that of others who have considered this issue, a complete new translation of English Collected Works is

---

150.   (1946), CW 8, § 421.
151.   (1954), CW 9, 1, § 45.
152.   (1932), CW 11, § 537.
153.   CW 18, § 1138.
154.   Bishop, 1998, p. 375.

highly desirable.[155] Finally the bibliography of Jung's writings is by no means complete.

As the project for the *Collected Works* proceeded, it came to include the publication of Jung's seminars and correspondence. In 1974, the *Freud–Jung Letters* were published, edited by William McGuire and Wolfgang Sauerlander. The editing of this edition was exemplary, and has set the standard for all subsequent volumes of Freud correspondences. A great deal of the subsequent secondary literature on the Freud–Jung relation has been largely parasitical on the information provided in the footnotes to this volume.

In 1973 and 1975, a selection of Jung's letters was published, edited by Gerhard Adler, in collaboration with Aniela Jaffé. The editors stated that, setting aside routine business letters from the 1,600 letters written by Jung between the years 1906 and 1961, they selected over 1,000.[156] This gives the impression that approximately two-thirds of the letters of Jung's that have survived were published in this volume. Furthermore, the publication of 196 letters of Jung to Freud in 1974 (only seven of which had appeared in the *Letters* volume) would leave only about 400 unpublished letters. This is seriously misleading. From my researches, I would estimate that the amount of Jung's letters represented in these volumes to be less than ten per cent. Moreover, their policy of only publishing Jung's letters and not that of his correspondents effectively decontexualized the letters that they did choose to include. From a comparison of the unpublished letters that I have read, problems in the choice of the letters that the editors selected are apparent. The larger share of the letters that the editors reproduced were from Jung's later years, and indeed, from the period when Aniela Jaffé was his secretary. Furthermore, the editors prioritized letters on religious subjects. Consequently, their edition by no means gives a fully representative portrait of Jung in correspondence.

The consequence of the shortcomings and unreliability of the *Collected Works* and *Letters* volumes is that one has, in effect, to

155. For a detailed study of the errors in one section of Hull's translation of Jung's "Theoretical reflections on the essence of the psychical", see David Holt, (1999).
156. Letters 1, p. xii.

"uncollect" the works, and start from basic primary research and comparison of manuscripts with first and subsequent editions, together with the study of complete correspondences.[157] Little of this work has been done. The reasons why such works should be published in proper historical editions is clear: for the quality of any field of thought is critically dependent on the comprehensiveness and reliability of its primary literature. Without such publications, secondary and tertiary literature on Jung will continue to based on unstable foundations.

In 1967, the Bollingen Foundation wound down and it transferred the US publication of Jung's works to Princeton University Press, leaving funds for the completion of the *Collected Works*. Under the terms of the agreement, unused funds would revert to Princeton University. In the 1990s the publication process ran aground, before even Jung's most important and extensive seminar lecture from 1932 to 1941 at the Swiss Federal Institute of Technology was published. In the late 1990s, Jung's *Collected Works* was declared closed by Princeton University Press, despite the extent of the unpublished works. A *Complete Works* of Jung remains a task for the future.[158]

---

157.   One instance where the first edition of a much revised text was recently reissued as part of the *Collected Works* in 1992 was Beatrice Hinkle's 1916 translation of *Transformations and Symbols of the Libido*. It has to be said that this reissue formed the low water mark of the *Collected Works*. On 10 April 1942, Jung wrote to Mary Mellon, "The 'Psychology of the Unconscious' should be translated again which it needs very badly indeed" (JA), orig in English. In January 1944, in response to a question from Stanley Young, Jung noted that the translation of the work should be revised. (BA). According to Joseph Henderson, Jung wanted the text retranslated, but ran into problems with the copyrights (personal communication). Later on, Richard Hull had wanted to retranslate the text, but was not given the go ahead. In 1964, Adler wrote to Read that "it is a well known fact that the Hinkle translation, on account of its lack of clarity and style, has done a great deal of harm to Jung's psychology, and I think its reissue in whatever form a grave mistake" (12 October 1964, RA).

158   In 2003, the Philemon Foundation was established to raise funds to accomplish this task. For details, see www.philemonfoundation.org.

CHAPTER THREE

Other lives

We turn now to biographies that were attempted after Jung's death. Were his subsequent biographers to prove any more successful at "catching the bird"? If Jung did not consider himself to be "fodder for the average sentimental needs of the general public", that did not deter others from considering him a suitable subject for trade biographies aimed at the general public. Morever, *Memories, Dreams, Reflections* had proved to be a massive bestseller, and indicated that there was indeed a large market for lives of Jung. Thus "Jung" became an attractive subject for professional biographers.

The following survey pays particular attention to the period which Jung called his "confrontation with the unconscious", which has possibly been the most mythologized aspect of Jung's life. From 1913 onwards, Jung engaged in a period of self-exploration, which has long been held to be central to the development of his later work. Before considering what has been made of this period, it is necessary to sketch some of the critical events that took place.

In his preface to the revised edition of *Transformations and Symbols of the Libido* in 1952, Jung recalled that shortly after writing the work (1912), he realized the significance of what it meant to live without a myth. As a result of this, he noted that

> I was driven to ask myself in all seriousness: "what is the myth you are living?" I found no answer to this question, and had to admit that I was not living with a myth, or even in a myth, but rather in an uncertain cloud of theoretical possibilities which I was beginning to regard with increasing distrust ... So in the most natural way, I took it upon myself to get to know "my" myth, and I regarded this as the task of tasks—for—so I told myself—how could I, when treating my patients, make due allowance for the personal factor, for my personal equation, which is yet so necessary for a knowledge of the other person, if I was unconscious of it?[159]

This question led Jung to undertake an extended period of self-experimentation. In the 1925 seminar, Jung narrated an event that occurred on a train journey to Schaffhausen in October 1913:

> I was travelling in a train and had a book in my hand that I was reading. I began to fantasize, and before I knew it, I was in the town to which I was going. This was the fantasy: I was looking down on the map of Europe in relief. I saw all the northern part, and England sinking down so that the sea came in upon it. It came up to Switzerland, and then I saw the mountains grew higher and higher to protect Switzerland. I realized that a frightful catastrophe was in progress, towns and people were destroyed, and the wrecks and dead bodies were tossing about on the water. Then the whole sea turned to blood. At first I was only looking on dispassionately, and then the sense of catastrophe gripped me with tremendous power. I tried to repress the fantasy, but it came up again and held me for two hours. Three or four weeks later it came again, when I was again in a train. It was the same picture repeated, only the blood was more emphasized.[160]

Jung did not understand what this meant at that time, and commented: "I had the feeling that I was an over-compensated psychosis, and from this feeling I was not released till August 1st,

---

159. Jung, *CW* 5, (1952), pp. 13–14. Bair misdated this episode to 1915 (2003, p. 255).
160. Jung, 1925, p. 41.

1914."[161] Jung initially viewed this waking fantasy subjectively and prospectively, ie., as depicting the imminent destruction of his world. When the first World War broke out, he thought that his fantasy had depicted not what would happen to *himself*, but to Europe.

Following this waking fantasy, Jung dedicated himself to a process of self-investigation. Until around 1900, he had kept a diary, and he took this up again as means of self observation.[162] He wrote down his fantasies which he studied. In studying his fantasies, he realized that he was studying the myth-creating function of the mind.

On 13 December, 1913, he decided to actively induce fantasies in a waking state. On the first occasion, he found himself in front of a dark cave. The entrance to the cave was blocked by a mummified dwarf, whom he squeezed past. He saw a red stone, which he tried to reach through muddy water. The stone covered an opening in the rock. Placing his ear to the opening, he heard a stream and saw a man who had been killed pass by, and also a black scarab. A red sun shone at the bottom of the stream, and there were snakes on the wall that crawled towards the sun, and eventually covered it. Blood sprang forth, and then subsided.[163] In retrospect, he commented:

> I realised of course, that it was a hero and solar myth, a drama of death and renewal, the rebirth symbolised by the Egyptian scarab. At the end, the dawn of the new day should have followed.[164]

Five days later, he had the important dream of killing Siegfried, which has been cited earlier.[165] He continued to invoke fantasies in a waking state. Shortly after, he had a series of fantasy encounters with the figures of Elijah and Salome.[166] Jung interpreted them in the following way: "Salome is an anima figure . . . Elijah is the personification of the cognitional element, Salome of the erotic . . . One could speak of these figures as the personifications of Logos

---

161. *Ibid.*, p. 44.
162. Protocols, LC, p. 23.
163. Jung, 1925, pp. 47–48; Jung/Jaffé, 1962, p. 203.
164. Jung/Jaffé, 1962, pp. 204–205. Cf. Jung, 1925, p. 62.
165. See above, p. 40.
166. Jung, 1925, pp. 63–64.

and Eros."[167] However, he immediately cautioned: "This is practical for intellectual play . . . but . . . it is very much better to leave the figures as they are, namely as events, experiences."[168] As we shall see, contrary to Jung's advice, many were to find such 'intellectual play' extremely appealing.

A critical figure in Jung's fantasies during this period was that of Philemon. In *Memories*, Jung recalled that Philemon first appeared to him in a dream. In this, Jung saw a sea blue sky, covered by brown clods of earth which appeared to be breaking apart. Out of the blue, he saw an old man with kingfisher wings and the horns of a bull flying across the sky, carrying a bunch of keys. After the dream, Jung painted the image, as he did not understand it. While he was doing this, he was struck to find a dead kingfisher at the bottom of his garden by the lakeshore, as kingfishers are rare around Zürich. Thereafter, Philemon played an important role in Jung's fantasies.[169] To Jung, he represented superior insight, and was like a guru to him. Jung would often converse with Philemon as he strolled in the garden of his home in Küsnacht. To Aniela Jaffé, he recalled, "He was simply a superior knowledge, and he taught me psychological objectivity and the actuality of the soul . . . He formulated and expressed everything which I had never thought."[170] Jung's fantasy figure was based on the figure of Philemon who had appeared in Ovid's Metamorphoses and in Goethe's *Faust*.

In addition to the biographers, this period has also attracted the attention of novelists and dramatists. Jung's waking fantasy of the catastrophic flood featured in Morris West's novel, *The World is Made of Glass*. West recast it as a dream, and added the following detail:

> Next I began to distinguish, among the dead, people I knew. Freud was there and Honegger and Emma and the children and my own father. I was oppressed with fear and shame because they were dead and I was alive and I did not want to leave the warm carriage and risk being drowned.[171]

---

167. *Ibid.*, p. 89.
168. *Ibid.*
169. Jung/Jaffé, 1962, p. 207.
170. Protocols, LC, pp. 23–24.
171. West 1983, p. 105.

West then presented a fictional account of Jung's analysis of this dream, and added this interpolation:

> Like every married man who has ever embarked on a love affair I have fantasies about being single and free again. My wife, my family, are obstacles to that freedom. My unconscious harbours the thought that, if they were to die, all my problems would be solved. Freud and my father are conjoined in another context. Father is dead. I am freed from his dominion. If Freud were dead I should inherit his mantle of authority.[172]

Here we see the Freudocentric legend of Jung even permeating the fantasies of novelists.

This waking fantasy also featured in Christopher Hampton's play, *The Talking Cure*, now as "recurring dream", which Jung narrated to Sabina Spielrein in the summer of 1913.

> SABINA: What do you think it means?
> JUNG: I've no idea: unless it is about to happen. Afterwards I feel sick; and ashamed. What are your plans?[173]

Jung didn't meet Spielrein in 1913, and this dialogue never happened.

The C. G. Jung Biographical Archive

After hearing of Jung's death, his student, the psychologist Henry Murray wrote to the analytical psychologist Frances Wickes that the "death of the great Old Man was like a cataclysm of Nature". Murray went on to pose the question,

> Is anybody in the world equal to the task of writing his biography? Perhaps some talented and devoted friend could—before it is too late—edit a preliminary collection or anthology of impressions or sketches by those who have been close to him or greatly benefited

---

172. *Ibid.*, p. 107.
173. Hampton 2002, p. 85. Findlay also added some embellishments to this fantasy (1999, p. 477).

by a few talks with him. Tape-recordings of memories of meetings with him might constitute a basis for a comprehensive biography to be written later.[174]

At the Harvard Psychological Clinic, Murray had pioneered the in-depth psychological investigation into individual lives. Wickes had intended to set aside a fund to further Jung's work, and after her death in 1967, the Wickes Foundation was established. Murray was one of the board members of the Foundation, and he took up the idea he had presented to Wickes years earlier.

In 1968, Murray approached a clinical psychologist, Gene Nameche, to see if he was interested to undertake a biographical project on Jung. Murray had chosen Nameche because he had heard good things about research on the study of lives, and he felt that it was important that the project be undertaken by someone who wasn't a Jungian. Murray had felt that a serious drawback of the interview project concerning Freud that had been conducted by the Sigmund Freud Archives was that the interviews had been conducted by a Freudian, namely, Kurt Eissler.[175]

The project was funded by the Wickes Foundation. The aim of the project was to interview people who had known Jung and record their memories. In the course of the project, Nameche noted that only six of the 205 people contacted for interviews refused.[176] Some of who refused gave interesting reasons for doing so.

Cary Baynes wrote to the Wickes Foundation declining to be interviewed for the book on Jung to be based on taped interviews of people who knew him:

> It is my conviction that this type of book is more likely to lead to a lesser, rather than a greater understanding of Jung. Each individual reporting will be able to speak only of a very limited aspect of Jung's character, because, to my way of thinking, no one, not even those closest to him, ever knew him as a whole. Moreover, too

---

174.   22 June 1961, Frances Wickes Collection, LC.

175.   Information from Gene Nameche, "The Origins of the C. G. Jung Biographical Archive", R. D. Laing archives, University of Glasgow. On the history of the Freud archives, see Borch-Jacobsen and Shamdasani, 2001.

176.   *Ibid.* On my count, the catalogue of the Countway library lists 152 different interviewees.

many years stand between me and the time I lived in Zürich, for me to feel competent to present a valid picture of Jung in that setting.[177]

Gerhard Adler also declined to be interviewed, giving two main reasons. First, he noted that in speaking of his relation with Jung, he would be reluctant to speak of his intimate experiences, but it was precisely such experiences which would be most revealing. He added that as an introvert, he would find more difficult more difficult to be interviewed than an extravert, and as this would generally be the case, the experiences narrated would be unbalanced. The most important reason was the following:

> my main objection is that there are too many projections and fantasy relations about. Too many people live with an image of their relationship to Jung which is utterly unreal. I do not see any way to distinguish between real and fantasy relationships.[178]

He added that the restrictions of ten or twenty years on consulting the interviews would actually make matters worse, as no one would be able to evaluate their reality or unreality.

In the early 1970s, 7,000 pages of transcriptions were placed in the Harvard Medical Archives, and the bulk of these interviews were made available in the 1980s. For Nameche, the goal of the interviews was to show the human side of Jung, and focus on personal contacts with him, as opposed to his ideas, and they largely succeeded in this.[179] As such, the interviews constitute an invaluable resource, but unfortunately, they were poorly conducted. In many cases, Nameche simply had not done enough homework to realize the historical significance of the figures he spoke to.[180] The interviews contain much gossip and rumours, and have to be used carefully. The problems highlighted by Cary Baynes and Gerhard Adler are clearly evident. The level of Nameche's

177.   Cary Baynes to Anne Phalon, 1 October 1969, McGuire papers, LC.
178.   Gerhard Adler to Hazard Gillespie, 16 September 1968, *Ibid*.
179.   Gene Nameche, "The origins of the C. G. Jung biographical archive", Laing archives.
180.   An example of this is his interview with Alphonse Maeder.

knowledge of Jung's work also left something to be desired.[181] However, in the main, Henry Murray's goal had indeed been fulfilled: the interviews constituted an essential resource for any future Jung biography. The bulk of the interviews became openly accessible in 1983.[182]

Ellenberger

1970 was a watershed in Jung's studies, as it saw the publication of Henri Ellenberger's *The Discovery of the Unconscious: The History and Evolution of Dynamic Psychiatry*. Though not properly speaking a biography, Ellenberger's work had critical implications for Jung biographies—which, regrettably, were not generally taken on board by the biographers.

Ellenberger was a psychiatrist of Swiss origin who worked at the University of Montreal, with a particular interest in phenomenological psychiatry. Though not a trained historian, Ellenberger's work was critical in the development of the history of psychiatry. Ellenberger had been analysed by Oskar Pfister, and he noted that the discrepancy between the accepted version of some events in the history of psychoanalysis and what he had directly heard from Pfister and from Alphonse Maeder was one of the instigators of his historical researches.[183] At the outset, he enunciated his methodology: "(1) Never take anything for granted. (2) Check everything. (3) Replace everything in its context. (4) Draw a sharp line of distinction between the facts and the interpretation of facts."[184]

---

181.   Nameche recounts how when he interviewed Jolande Jacobi in 1969, she said to him: "'Of course, Dr. Nameche, you have read all the works of Jung.' I answered, 'I have read in all the works of Jung.' She laughed heartily." *Jung and Persons: A Study in Genius and Madness*, R. D. Laing papers, University of Glasgow, p. 166.

182.   When the Wickes Foundation was wound down, a terminal grant was given to the C. G. Jung Institute of San Francisco. A grant of $5,000 was also given to the Sigmund Freud Archives for the acquisition of Freud letters (Kurt Eissler to William McGuire, 8 May 1970, McGuire papers, LC).

183.   Ellenberger, 1970a, p. xiv. On Ellenberger, see Mark Micale's introduction to Ellenberger, 1993.

184.   *Ibid.*, p. v.

He enlarged upon this in an essay published in the same year entitled, "Methodology in writing the history of dynamic psychiatry", His goal was to locate the history of dynamic psychiatry solidly within the discipline of history. He commenced this by noting that the average dynamic psychiatrist was not trained in historical methods and did not have historical knowledge, and was likely to be the adherent of a particular school. Concerning the latter, he argued that:

> To have undergone a Freudian or Jungian analysis, or any such training, is a definite advantage, but can also be a severe handicap for the historian. Not infrequently, the adherents of a particular school will view the teachings of other schools in a distorted fashion even when they believe themselves to be impartial. Here, the historian should "put between brackets" all he knows about his own school and should endeavor to identify himself with the object of his study in order to reconstruct the teaching of another school, in the same way as the psychiatric phenomenologist strives to reconstruct piece by piece the inner universe of a schizophrenic patient.[185]

This statement indicates the significance of a quasi-phenomenological perspective for Ellenberger's historiography. He insisted that one should scrupulously check biographical data, one should study works in a chronological order, never rely on translations, and always read the first editions and not the collected works of an author. From the standpoint of the discipline of history, such a methodology would appear to be elementary and could be taken for granted. However, within a domain dominated by legends, rumour and gossip, such an emphasis on documentary evidence and primary sources was revolutionary. He concluded that such a methodology, though time-consuming, would "produce works definitely more rewarding that those based on second-, third-, or fourth-hand material, repeating indefinitely the same errors which have never been questioned and have acquired an unfortunate appearance of veracity".[186]

---

185. Ellenberger, 1970b, pp. 34–35.
186. *Ibid.*, p. 39.

Ellenberger devoted lengthy chapters to Janet, Freud, Adler, and Jung. For the first time, Jung's work was presented in context of the history of ideas, and was not subsumed under or subordinated to psychoanalysis. His chapter on Jung, which is well over a hundred pages, began with the opening statement:

> Carl Gustav Jung, no more than Alfred Adler, is a deviant from Freud's psychoanalysis, and his analytic psychology should not be measured with the yardstick of Freudian psychoanalysis any more than psychoanalysis should be measured with the yardstick of analytic psychology. Both should be understood in terms of their own philosophy.[187]

It is no great exaggeration to say that this statement could be said to mark the inception of the field of Jung history as a distinct domain.[188] Ellenberger's work accomplished two tasks: the separation of Jung from the shadow of Freud, and at the same time, the reconnection of Jung's work within a wider field of relations to other developments and contemporaneous developments. The significance of Ellenberger's account of Jung's life was that it gave prominence to his ideas and the evolution of his work. Critically, the study of Jung's life was embedded in a vast recontextualization of the history of dynamic psychiatry. While Ellenberger commenced archival investigations into Jung's life, the status of *Memories* was unquestioned.

Conceptually, Ellenberger's work combined the approaches of a historian and that of an existential psychiatrist, and there are at times tensions between these orientations. One specific idea was prominent in his treatment of Jung, namely, the concept of the "creative illness". In 1964, he wrote an essay on this topic, taking his cue from Novalis, who had remarked,

> Illnesses are certainly an important matter for humanity, since they are so numerous and because everyone has to struggle against them. But we know only imperfectly the art of putting them to

---

187.   Ellenberger 1970a, p. 657.
188.   See Eugene Taylor, 1996. Possibly the first historical monograph was James Heisig's exemplary study, *Imago Dei: A Study of Jung's Psychology of Religion* (1979).

good use. These are probably the most important materials and stimulants for our thinking and activity.[189]

Ellenberger posed the question as to whether one could find historical examples of creative processes hidden under "the appearance or disappearance of a neurosis or psychosomatic illness?" He provided the following general schema of the "creative illness": the illness commences after a period of intense intellectual effort, during the illness, the subject is obsessed with an intellectual, spiritual, or aesthetic problem. The termination of illness is experienced as not only the liberation from a period of psychological suffering, but also as an illumination. Finally, this is followed by a transformation of the personality, and often with gaining followers. He cited examples among the shamans and religious mystics, and also notably, Freud and Jung. The latter, he maintained, had "suffered from a kind of protracted neurotic disorder", after his break with Freud. Ellenberger maintained that "the essential features of Jung's teaching, therefore, are the result of his creative neurosis".[190] The "creative illness" was an ambiguous term. It did not challenge the diagnoses of the episodes in question as "illnesses", but attempted to indicate that there were also creative processes involved. Unfortunately, while Ellenberger's history of dynamic psychiatry opened up a great number of critical sources for the contextual study of Jung's work, the concept of the creative illness acted in the opposite direction, telescoping down into Jung's "creative neurosis".

After Ellenberger, an increasing number of historical studies of Jung and aspects of the development of his work took place by scholars in a variety of disciplines, in the form of monographs, articles and dissertations. These works were linked to a complete rewriting of the history of psychiatry, psychoanalysis, psychology and psychotherapy, and the human sciences that was under way at the same time. However, such works were dispersed, and made little impression on the profession of analytical psychology and the wider public discussion of Jung. Furthermore, such studies had

---

189.   Ellenberger, 1993, cited, p. 328. On illness in German Romanticism, see David Krell, 1998.

190.   *Ibid.*, p 339.

little effect on the continued attempts to write biographies of Jung, which underwent a separate development. Regrettably, the general historical methodology which Ellenberger promoted was by no means always adhered to in the Jung biographical tradition.

Jung: His Life and Work

In 1976, Barbara Hannah published her work, *Jung: His Life and Work. A Biographical Memoir*. Hannah was a painter and had come to Zürich at the beginning of 1929 to work with Jung.[191] She remained in Switzerland, and practised as an analyst. In the 1930s, she prepared a several volume résumé of Jung's lectures at the Federal Institute of Technology, and also translated some of his writings.[192]

In the preface to her book, she stated that as a biographical memoir, her aim was to show Jung's life as it appeared to her. She felt that it was too early for a detailed biography, as there were many documents held by the Jung family which were not yet accessible for study. She admitted that she knew little of Jung's family life, but was approaching it solely from her own standpoint, that is, of a student who also knew him outside of analysis. Her aim was to show how he "first lived his psychology and only much later formulated in words what he had lived"[193] Thus, her focus was on his own process of individuation. A subsidiary aim was to put on record information that might otherwise subsequently die with her, and in particular, concerning his relationship with Toni Wolff. In a paper written in 1967, "Some glimpses of the individuation process in Jung himself", Hannah noted that Jung's continued presence in people's dreams and active imaginations "gives us the sense of his near presence", and rendered his death less of an "icy barrier" than

---

191.   Hannah 1976, pp. 190–191.
192.   Bair described Barbara Hannah as a lesbian (Bair, 2003, p. 364). Emmanuel Kennedy, Hannah's literary executor, who has her diaries, stated that this is not true. He also noted that many of Bair's descriptions of Hannah are derogatory (personal communication).
193.   *Ibid.*, p. 7.

that of others that she had been affected by.[194] There is a sense in which her biography seeks to evoke this sense of presence.

In the early chapters of her book, she drew heavily on *Memories, Dreams, Reflections*, supplemented with anecdotes that Jung narrated to her, and things she had heard from other people. The work qualitatively changes after the time Hannah herself came to Zürich in the 1920s, given her presence at some of the events she narrated, her acquaintances with other figures in Jung's circle, and the manner in which she took note of comments made by Jung. Hannah's account of his "confrontation with the unconscious" faithfully followed the account in *Memories*, supplemented by comments that Jung made to Hannah. Though not a scholarly study or a professional work of history, Hannah's work drew on a lifetime's involvement with Jung's psychology. It contains invaluable first-hand information. However, it is not always possible to evaluate the veracity of her accounts.[195] If the book does contain unverified gossip, it is at least first-hand gossip, which has not been subjected to decades of elaboration. As a "biographical memoir", Hannah's work is restricted in what it sets out to do, but this restriction proves to be its strength. As such I regard it as still the only indispensable biography of Jung. Subsequent biographies have only heightened its significance.

In assessing these works, it is important to look at the narrative conventions employed. Of the "posthumous" biographers, Hannah could draw upon years of direct contact with Jung in preparing her book, and phrases like "Jung told me" occur frequently. The same does not hold for the next batch of biographers. As we saw in the case of *Memories*, a first person narrative contributed greatly to a particular account being taken as definitive. In the works we now turn to, we see how in a lesser way, third person narratives could still be used in a manner which gives the impression that the biography in question presents a window into Jung's intimate thoughts —even without documentary evidence.

---

194. Hannah, 1967, p. 10.
195. One individual who was critical of this aspect of her study was the late C. A. Meier. He commented that Hannah wrote of things which she couldn't possibly know (personal communication).

C. G. Jung: The Haunted Prophet

In 1976, the psychotherapist Paul Stern published a biography of Jung entitled, *C. G. Jung: The Haunted Prophet*. Stern's approach was avowedly critical. In his view, Jung was a "seer" disguised as a scientist. Stern regarded *Memories* as "a self-conscious gospel and Bible of the Jungian dispensation, in the form of a parable",[196] and the Jung Institute in Zürich as Jung's "mystical body". Stern viewed Jung's life story as "a compelling parable that illustrates the creative uses of incipient madness".[197] Stern's work is poorly referenced and did not have any footnote references. It seems to include some information which may have come from Nameche's interviews.

It is significant to note that it appears that the first to claim that Jung was mad—in some form or other—were the psychoanalysts. Their position is quite clear: Jung's so-called madness was used to explain his defection from psychoanalysis. Consequently, his work could simply be dismissed as the product of a psychosis. For example, on 9 December 1912 Freud wrote to Sándor Ferenczi, "Jung is crazy [meschugge]".[198] A few months later, he used a similar expression in a letter to Karl Abraham.[199] On 25 April 1913, Ernest Jones wrote to Freud that Jung's

> recent conduct in America makes me think more than [ever] that he does not react like a normal man, and that he is mentally deranged to a serious extent; he produced quite a paranoiac impression on some of the ψα psychiatrists in Ward's Island.[200]

How else to explain Jung's apostasy from the Freudian Cause, except by invoking madness? After Freud, this view was repeated by psychoanalysts and has had a major propaganda effect. In 1982, Eissler published an essay entitled, "Beginnings of a pathography of C. G. Jung's personality", which is an example of psychoanalytic character assassination, where it is quite clear that diagnosing Jung was a way of discrediting his ideas.[201]

---

196. Stern, 1976, p. 17.
197. *Ibid.*, p. 9.
198. Falzeder, Brabant, and Giampieri-Deutsch, 1993, p. 440.
199. "Jung is crazy [verrückt]", 1 June 1913, Falzeder, 2002, p. 186.
200. Paskauskas, 1993, p. 1999.

Stern viewed Jung's 'confrontation with the unconscious' as "the years of semi-psychosis".[202] In his view, Jung's solution to his crisis was that he "personalised and mythologised the psychotic forces within him".[203] Thus, for Stern, Jung's life demonstrates the birth of a psychology out of a psychosis, and the manner in which Jung constructed it is sufficient to repudiate it. Stern's reading did not focus on the meaning of particular events, but on the general tendencies of Jung that he maintained they demonstrated. In his comments on Jung's Siegfried dream, Stern wrote that Jung:

> failed to see how solipsistic and "Jungian" his interpretation actually was. He had fallen into the trap that invariably dooms attempts at self-analysis, seeing in the dream only what he wanted to see. Oblivious to his blind spot, caught in a narrow world of shadows, viewing each dream image as merely another facet of himself, he was able to mitigate the terrible impact of outer reality—at the price of reducing his contact with it.[204]

Stern viewed the figure of Philemon as representing what Jung had "looked for, apparently found, and then tragically lost in Freud: paternal guidance, readiness to minister to his spiritual needs".[205] However, Stern does credit Jung with managing to overcome his ordeal:

> The figure of Carl Jung is living proof that even in the twentieth century a person can be a visionary, "hallucinating" ghosts and demons, without being manifestly mad. Therein lies part of his importance for us now.[206]

---

201. Eissler, 1982. It is important to note that it was not only Jung's critics who held this view. For example we find Anthony Storr claiming that Jung went through a 'psychotic episode' and suffered from 'grandiose delusions' (Storr, 1997, p. 89, p. 91).
202. Stern, 1976, p. 156.
203. Ibid., p. 10.
204. Ibid., p. 120.
205. Ibid., p. 122.
206. Ibid., p.120.

Stern does not pay attention to the social and intellectual context of Jung's work. His overall judgement on Jung and his work is damning:

> In the intellectual realm, Jung's great synthesis remained very much at the level of mere verbal operations whose superficialities were concealed by an impressive array of erudition. Jung's often-noted lack of lucidity, his turgid style, the leakiness of his logic, his inability to distinguish between hypotheses and facts are as many telltale signs of this lack of integration. And the biographical facts we have chronicled at some length reflect the same failure in the existential realm.[207]

Criticisms of how Jung lived his life joins together with a dismissal of his work, without even entering into any detailed consideration of it. Thus, biography provided a simple way for a global criticism of Jung.

Jung: Man and Myth

In 1978, Vincent Brome, a professional biographer, published his biography, *Jung: Man and Myth*. According to the cover blurb, the book "reveals to us the truth behind the myth of the semi-mystical Messiah". Brome, who had met Jung on two occasions, interviewed about thirty people who had known Jung. Among those he interviewed were some individuals whom he did not name. At the outset, Brome stated his book was not a definitive work, which he considered we would have to wait another thirty years for.[208] For his account of Jung's early and late years, Brome drew heavily on *Memories, Dreams, Reflections*, unaware of its problematic status. Brome's attitude towards Jung's work is clear in an appendix on "Jung's model of the psyche", where he presented an outline of Jung's ideas, which he critiqued. Brome is far more sympathetic to psychoanalysis, and presented Freudian interpretations of Jung.[209]

---

207. *Ibid.*, pp. 256–257.
208. Brome, 1978, p. 12.
209. One example is Brome's interpretation of Jung's oedipal complex, *ibid.*, p. 35.

Hence Brome's approach can be characterized as psychobiographical, rather than historical. Brome encapsulated his overall assessment of Jung's work in the following statement:

> There was a sense in which Jung's model of the human psyche converted autobiography into psychotherapy. He had experienced every detail of his model, and it was as if he had elevated an elaborate process of self-analysis into abstract theory convinced that it had universal application.[210]

If one holds such a position, it follows that a biography of Jung would present the key to an understanding of his work and its genesis. Such a position negates intellectual history.

Brome's psychobiographical approach is particularly apparent in his version of Jung's "confrontation with the unconscious", which he understood as a "breakdown". To be more precise, Brome diagnosed Jung as "a cyclothymic personality who suffered a manic depressive psychosis", and raises the question whether hereditary factors were present in Jung's "illness".[211]

Brome challenged Jung's statements that his self-exploration was a deliberately undertaken enterprise:

> Just how far deliberation entered into the process, and to what degree pathological forces carried him involuntarily back to his beginnings is difficult to establish ... with a psyche so complex, rich and powerful every conceivable complication cross-fertilised the process until the rationally willed was indistinguishable from the compulsively inescapable.[212]

Jung's critical dreams and fantasies were subjected to reductive interpretations. We may see this by considering his treatment of Jung's "confrontation with the unconscious".

Brome interpreted Jung's waking fantasy of 13 December 1913 and dream of Siegfried cited earlier from the perspective of Jung's "traumatic" break with Freud. Concerning the first, he commented:

210.   *Ibid.*, p. 284.
211.   *Ibid.*, p. 168, p. 162.
212.   *Ibid.*, p. 158.

Jung was six foot, Freud five feet seven, one relatively a dwarf to the other, and there in the first dream, the entrance to the cave was blocked by a mummified dwarf. The dead Freud checked Jung's struggle towards rebirth so powerfully that when the sun of a new day arose in the cave it suddenly obliterated everything with a bursting jet of blood, simultaneously symbolising rebirth and death.[213]

Brome interpreted the Siegfried dream in terms of Jung's supposed "identification" with Freud.[214] He set Jung's own interpretations of the fantasy and the dream in *Memories* to one side. His approach was to view Jung's experiences during this period in terms of interpersonal dynamics. His overall interpretation of Jung's confrontation with the unconscious boils down to the following:

> Slowly the reasonably "normal", conventionally faithful married man, believing in one form of God, had been revealed as a person with bi-sexual potential, committing adultery, unreconciled to the personal God of Christianity and capable of murdering his own father [ie., Freud] at one remove.[215]

The misprison of the Freudocentric reading of Jung is readily apparent in this account. Furthermore, one sees how psychoanalytic interpretations are used to insert "Freud" into texts from which he is completely absent. Jung "must" have been preoccupied with Freud at this time, therefore these experiences "must" have been about his relation to Freud. Besides, what evidence is there that Jung was actually *capable of murdering Freud*, aside from the imputation of Oedipal hostility? The problem with such interpretations is that they are completely arbitrary. If one employs such hermeneutics, anything can stand for anything, without the need for any supportive evidence.[216]

---

213. *Ibid.*, p. 163.
214. For Kurt Eissler, Siegfried was a son figure, and hence represented Franz Jung, who, according to Eissler, was at the height of his Oedipal phase (1982, p. 119). Robert Smith notes that "Nearly all psychoanalytic interpreters have drawn a direct and explicit connection between SIGmund Freud and SieGfried" (1997, p. 64).
215. Brome, 1978, p. 168.
216. The first to posit that Jung had a "death-wish" against Freud was Freud himself when they met at Bremen in 1909, as an interpretation of Jung's

In historical work, as opposed to journalism, it is crucial that references and sources are clearly given, for this is the only way in which other scholars can potentially assess the reliability of the material in question and the claims made about it. A feature of Brome's book is his reliance on anonymous sources. Information concerning Jung's monetary discussions with his wife during his honeymoon is credited to an "anonymous English psychiatrist".[217] An event where Jung allegedly awoke at night to hear his youngest daughter crying and left to seek solace with Toni Wolff is credited to an interview with "X".[218] Brome referred to an anonymous person who talked to him "under a heavy cloak of anonymity with nothing more than corroborative verbal evidence from similar sources."[219] The web of intrigue thickens—we now have anonymous sources backing up other anonymous sources. Brome judiciously stated that it would be a mistake to take these as reliable, but then in the same sentence goes on to present another anonymous witness "who knew the situation intimately described him [Jung] as not a great lover. His sexuality was very straightforward, and all the mythopoeic talk vanished in a cloud of uncomplicated passion".[220] Talk of sexuality and anonymity often appear to go hand in hand. We are left with no way to evaluate the veracity of these accounts, nor to ascertain to what extent they are based on first-, second- or third-hand evidence, nor to judge the reliability of

interest in the corpses recently found there (Jones, 1955, p. 166). Jung commented to Bennet, "I had branded myself, in becoming identified with Freud. Why should I want him to die? I had come to learn. He was not standing in my way: he was in Vienna, I was in Zürich. Freud identified himself with his theory—in this case, his theory of the old man of the tribe whose death every young man must want; the son must want to displace the father. But Freud wasn't my father!" (Bennet 1961, p. 44). According to Jones, it was at Bremen that Jung was persuaded to have his first alcoholic drink since leaving the Burghölzli, with its teetotal regime (1955, pp. 61, 165). This point is repeated by Paul Roazen (1974, p. 246), McLynn (1996, p. 135), and Bair (2003, p. 161). However, in commenting on Jones' biography, Jung pointed out to Bennet that this was mistaken, and that he had celebrated leaving the Burghölzli by drinking (Bennet, diary, 18 September, 1959, Bennet papers, ETH).

217. Brome, 1978, p. 83.
218. *Ibid.*, p. 170.
219. *Ibid.*
220. *Ibid.*

the witnesses. In the case of Jung, given the level of fantasy and gossip that surrounded him since his early days at the Burghölzli, this presents an especial problem. As we have seen, it was for these types of reasons that Cary Baynes and Gerhard Adler declined to be interviewed for the Jung biographical project.

Brome presented information from a woman who had been a patient of Jung and who insisted on anonymity, whom he called "Anna Maria". Anna Maria was an English woman, who had been sent to Jung at eighteen, suffering from anorexia. Brome commented, "the case is particularly interesting because Jung developed his new—mythological—analysis with this patient".[221] If this was the case, this patient would be a vitally important paradigm case, but we are not even given the dates as to when the analysis took place. Without these details, such information is unusable from a historical perspective.

"Jung and Persons: A Study in Genius and Madness"

In 1983, Nameche completed the manuscript of a short biography of Jung, written with R. D. Laing, entitled: "Jung and Persons: A Study in Genius and Madness". The work was never published. The focus of the work was Jung's relationships with others. In the introduction, Laing and Nameche wrote:

> we offer this book, as a contribution to remembrance, Platonic and Freudian, forgiveness, reconciliation, and, even, celebration, of the existence of a great human spirit, who was not a saint, and was not a pig, but was an incorrigible man. As the Mexicans say, a man is rare.[222]

They indicated the requirements incumbent upon any one embarking upon a biography of Jung:

> To go the whole way, negatively, on Jung, however, one has to earn one's rank. Maybe he is a fool, a charlatan, a complete bastard. But

---

221. *Ibid.*, p. 178.
222. R. D. Laing papers, University of Glasgow, p. iv.

to be entitled to make such judgements, one has to do his home-work, a lot of one's own, and at least be in a position to appreciate what he was going on about. He was certainly not going on about total nonsense, as some people are stupid enough to suppose, and many others would like to be believe.[223]

The following is a list of the chapters of the work:

1. Ancestors and Ghosts from the Past
    Heritage and Heresy

2. Fundamentals of Early Experience 1875–1902
    From Parsonage to Personage

3. Young Dr. Jung 1903–1912
    Freud, Family and Fame

4. Mid-life Reorientations 1913–1925
    Breaking-down, in and out

5. Getting Id Together 1926–1945
    Travel and Honours; War and Worries

6. Jung Around Men
    Jealousies, Dis-grace and Fidelity

7. Women Around Jung
    The Two Choirs: Saving Grace?

8. Old Doctor Jung 1946–1961
        Losses, Fame and Carving in Stone

Apart from occasional insights, the Laing/Nameche biography is a disappointing work, having little of the brilliance of the former, nor of the research of the latter. Indeed, by the time he came to write this, Nameche appears to have forgotten much of the information from his interviews. The work in no way represents the culmination of his interview project.[224]

---

223. *Ibid.*, p. iii.
224. In 1984, Colin Wilson published a short book entitled, *C. G. Jung: Lord of the Underworld*. Once again, we find that this work presents a reading of Jung cast in the frame of the narration of his life, the details of which, in this case, are provided by *Memories, Dreams, Reflections*, and supplemented by Brome's biography.

Jung: A Biography

In 1985, Gerhard Wehr published a work on Jung entitled, *Carl Gustav Jung: Life, Work, Effect*, which was translated as *Jung: A Biography*. Unlike the professional biographers, Wehr had previously written on the religious aspects of Jung's thought. In 1972, he wrote a comparative study of Jung and Rudolf Steiner (Wehr, 1972). In 1975, he published a work on the relations of Jung's work to Christianity, with the intention of seeing how analytical psychology could contribute to a "depth theology". (Wehr, 1975). Thus his work arose out of a sustained involvement with Jung's thought.

Unlike the biographies which preceded it, it did not present any new archival material or draw on interviews with individuals who knew Jung. Wehr relied heavily on *Memories, Dreams, Reflections*, which was uncritically taken as Jung's biography. After considering Brome's work, it comes a relief to find an absence of psychobiographical interpretation. Instead, Wehr presented Jung's own accounts of his experience, and showed a firm grasp of his ideas.[225] Wehr relied on material that had already been published. Thus, if there is little new in Wehr's book to make it stand out, it is also free of the many of the flaws of some of the earlier biographies of Jung, and generally known facts are reliably narrated.

In considering Jung's "confrontation with the unconscious", Wehr's account faithfully followed that in *Memories*, supplemented by information from Hannah's biography. Wehr added his own diagnosis of Jung as "'a borderline case' on the threshold between neurosis and psychosis".[226] Wehr raised the question of whether Jung's undertaking was indeed voluntary, or whether it was his "inner conflicts" which "were driving him to the edge of insanity".[227] However, he added that such an experience could not be understood in psychopathological criteria alone, but rather should also be seen as an example of the archetypal "night sea journey", invoking Jung's 1912 *Transformations and Symbols of the Libido*.[228] He

---

225. In 1969 Wehr also published an illustrated portrait of Jung, which contained an number of hitherto unpublished pictures, including some of Jung's paintings.

226. Wehr, 1985, p. 175.

227. *Ibid.*

228. *Ibid.*, p. 177.

also suggested there were parallels to Jung's experience in the history of Christian esotericism. Concerning Jung's dream of killing Siegfried, Wehr added to Jung's own interpretation the fact that "many of his Jewish colleagues had once looked upon him as just such 'gigantic blond Siegfried'" and that "Siegfried was also the name of the son whom Sabina Spielrein longed for".[229] Wehr's biography concludes with three short essays that survey the cultural reception of Jung's work, particularly in religious circles.

Carl Gustav Jung: A Biography

In 1996, Frank McLynn, another professional biographer, published his biography of Jung. At the outset, he stated that his book "does not purport to be a definitive biography of Jung. Such a work will not be possible until all the relevant documentation is released into the public domain".[230] If the last sentence seems to present an appropriately cautious position, it is cancelled out by the statement which follows: "Nevertheless, I would be surprised if future discoveries significantly alter our perception of Jung's doctrines and their implications".[231] How is McLynn in a position to know the insignificance of what he has not read? He nevertheless expressed his certainty that future research would reveal the names of Jung's "unknown" mistresses, and the dates of their liaisons.[232] He added that due to the controversies around Jung's work, he did not "seek expert advice or academic readings" so as not to "absorb any of the conscious or unconscious *parti pris* the man and his doctrines provoke".[233] No new research on Jung is presented. Instead, we have the mirror opposite of Wehr: instead of a respectful tracing of known events in Jung's life and Jung's own interpretations of them, McLynn is harshly critical of Jung.

McLynn regarded *Memories* uncritically, and this led him to make rash judgements. He claimed that "Jung did not, in any

---

229. *Ibid.*, p. 180.
230. McLynn, 1995, p. ix.
231. *Ibid.*
232. *Ibid.*
233. *Ibid.*, p. x.

significant sense of the word love Emma [his wife]. This fact might be inferred, as Anthony Storr suggests, from the simple fact that Emma is mentioned just twice, in entirely trivial contexts, in Memories".[234] Similarly, he interpreted the lack of mention of Bleuler as follows: "Jung's anger towards his father, it seems, was visited on all successive 'father figures'".[235] However, in the protocols of Jung's interviews with Jaffé for *Memories*, there were several significant comments concerning his wife and Bleuler, which cause McLynn's fantastic extrapolations to collapse.

Far from avoiding *parti pris*, this work epitomized the prevalent Freudocentric view of Jung. This perspective is clearly apparent in his reading of Jung's "confrontation with the unconscious", which he viewed as "a general process of mental disintegration which took him to the edge of the abyss".[236] For McLynn, Jung had a "mental illness". In McLynn's account of Jung, everything revolves around Freud. The biographer's *idée fixe* becomes attributed to Jung. This is apparent in his reading of Jung's Siegfried dream: "Once again Jung shied away from the obvious meaning. It is a commonplace of Jungian hermeneutics that Siegfried stands for Freud and that the murder and guilt represent Jung's 'parricide'."[237] McLynn claimed that Salome stood for Toni Wolff, though he left open the possibility that she may also have stood for Lou-Andreas Salomé.[238]

Concerning Jung's Philemon, McLynn categorically stated that "the entire Philemon experience was a schizophrenic episode, a psychotic symptom in no essential way different from the delusions and voices perceived by the Burghölzli patients".[239] McLynn looked at Jung's painting of Philemon and could only see Freud.[240] Hence,

---

234. *Ibid.*, p. 83.
235. *Ibid.*, p. 57.
236. *Ibid.*, p. 233.
237. *Ibid.*, p. 237. One assumes that McLynn meant "Freudian" hermeneutics.
238. *Ibid.*
239. *Ibid.*, p. 239.
240. *Ibid.*, p. 240. For Kurt Eissler, Philemon was an "Ersatz" for Freud. (1982, p. 121). For Susan Rowland, Philemon "may be connected to both Jung's own father and Freud" (1999, p. 46).

Philemon can be considered "as a Janus figure: at once a sign of Jung's regaining his own authority ... after destroying Freud/ Siegfried and a prefiguring of his emphasis on the tasks of the second half of life, when gurus and wise old men come into their own".[241]

Like Stern, McLynn regarded Jung as a prophet masquerading as a scientist: "Acres of print could have been saved if Jung had come clean and admitted that he was a prophet".[242] He regarded Jung's work as being "far from intellectually coherent".[243] However, one can question the level of his familiarity with it. For example, Jung, he claimed, was "never much interested in child psychology".[244]. Consequently, he concluded, "Perhaps the most serious defect in Jung's psychology is the lack of any theory or analysis of childhood".[245] However, Jung conducted detailed investigations into children's dreams, on which he held a seminar lasting several years, published in German in 1987.[246]

Regarding Jung' love life, McLynn felt free to nominate mistresses at will. He explained Jung's warning to Sabina Spielrein about meeting Mira Gincburg by claiming "presumably she was yet another of Jung's mistresses whose revelations could be embarrassing".[247] No evidence is provided to support this claim. McLynn simply stated that Fräulein Aptekmann and Martha Boddinghaus were also mistresses of Jung, without providing any evidence.[248] The image of Jung that emerges in this work is that of a psychotic philanderer. Regrettably, this image is not confined to McLynn's biography.

---

241. *Ibid.*
242. *Ibid.*, p. 316.
243. *Ibid.*, p. 311.
244. *Ibid.*, p. 103.
245. *Ibid.*, p. 314.
246. An English edition is currently in preparation.
247. *Ibid.*, p. 113.
248. *Ibid.*, p. 161. In a letter to Freud of 8 September 1910, Jung noted that there was a "loving jealously over me" between Moltzer and Boddinghaus (McGuire, 1974, p. 352).

A Life of Jung

In 1999, Ronald Hayman, another professional biographer, published his biography of Jung, *A Life of Jung*. Hayman was the first biographer who was aware of the status of *Memories, Dreams, Reflections*, and drew on the protocols of Aniela Jaffé's interviews with Jung. Furthermore, he was the first biographer to draw on the Countway interviews, supplemented with some interviews of his own. Of the biographers of Jung to date, Hayman devoted the most space, comparatively speaking, to giving summaries of Jung's actual writings. Also, he did not rely on existing translations of Jung's works, and sometimes revised existing translations and supplied his own. Like the previous biographers, Hayman did not consult the Jung archives in Zürich.

Like Stern, Brome and McLynn before him, Hayman presented his own retrospective analysis of Jung. This is particularly marked in his account of Jung's "confrontation with the unconscious", which he regarded as a breakdown. Hayman employed Ellenberger's rubric of the "creative illness", but went further in stressing what he considered to be the psychopathological nature of Jung's experiences. In his reading of Jung's Siegfried dream, Hayman contended that Jung's "need to keep silent" about Sabina Spielrein stopped him from "writing honestly about this dream", as Siegfried obviously signified Spielrein's Siegfried fantasy—a connection which had been posited by Wehr.[249] The assumption that one knows what this dream "really meant" led to the claim that Jung did not write honestly about it. Like Brome and McLynn, Hayman saw Freud as the critical figure in Jung's "confrontation with the unconscious". In his discussion of the figures of Salome and Elijah, he noted:

> One factor in his disorientation was the loss of the people who mattered to him most—Freud and Sabina. Both Jewish, they could be both be associated with the Old Testament. Though he was to speculate at length about the meaning of Salome and Elijah—pointing out that in myth an old man is often accompanied by a young girl who represents the erotic while he represents wisdom—he

---

249. Hayman, 1999, p. 176.

never made the obvious equations. . . . Like dissidents who have
been eliminated in a Soviet purge and vanish from new prints of
old photographs, they are mentioned in none of Jung's accounts of
his dreams and visions. It was as he had forbidden himself to think
about them. . . . Perhaps he saw it but he did not dare to admit he
was conflating Sabina with Lou Andreas-Salomé.[250]

Nowhere is evidence provided for such claims.[251] Hayman's interpretations are taken as facts, and he gives the impression of know-
ing the hidden content of Jung's mind. Regarding Jung's own
interpretations of his experience, Hayman argued that Jung
"always tended to mythologise his experience, and now he was
verging on psychosis, Gnosticism gave him a kind of licence".[252] It
is striking how many commentators have reinterpreted Jung's
fantasies in terms of people in his life, leaving to one side his own
interpretations of them in terms of subjective tendencies or functions of his personality. Jung's tendency to personification, such as
in the figure of Philemon, Hayman read in terms of the tendencies
of schizophrenics.[253] He attributed "delusions of grandeur" to Jung.
Furthermore, central features of Jung's work are attributed to such
tendencies: "His inclination to believe in what he called the inde-
pendence of the unconscious is in line with his boyhood refusal to
accept responsibility for such images as the giant penis and the
divine turd."[254] Psychobiography thus becomes a tool of criticism.
Jung becomes remade according to each biographer's fixed ideas.

Critically, none of the biographies discussed in this chapter
drew upon Jung's extensive unpublished manuscripts and notes,

---

251. In my view, Jung's family meant considerably more to him than
Freud or Spielrein. This mythology is proving to be stubbornly long lived. In his
novel, *The World is Made of Glass*, Morris West wrote: "Salome . . . is the hostile
woman playing the role of the naked seductress to me, a man who has no desire
for her. There is a clear connection to Sabina Spielrein, who I thought had written her way out of my life for good" (West, 1983, p. 131). We find Susan
Rowland claiming that "A number of studies have noticed what Jung appeared
not to, that in Elijah and Salome, he had versions of the two important people
he had just lost, Freud and Sabina Spielrein" (2002, p. 9). Rowland cited F-X.
Charet, John Kerr, and Hayman.
252. Hayman, 1999, p. 178.
253. *Ibid.*, pp. 178–179.
254. *Ibid.*, p. 60.

nor on his voluminous correspondence at the ETH. These are available for scholars to study upon application. Nor did any of the biographers have access to the Jung family archives, which contains private materials, such as Jung's correspondence with his wife, the *Black Books*, and the *Red Book*. Thus, the most important unpublished materials remained unexamined.[255]

Confronted by this situation, one could simply base oneself on what is known, and be careful not to overstep the bounds of the available documentation.

The works of Hannah and Wehr can generally be seen to fall into this category. On the other hand, there is the danger of filling in the gaps of the available information with intreprefactions. The works of Stern, McLynn, Brome, and Hayman at times fall into this category.

---

255. This situation has dissuaded some individuals from undertaking a biography of Jung: for example, in the late 1980s, William McGuire had considered writing a Jung biography. As the Jung family were not willing to co-operate to the extent to which he requested, he decided against the project, as he felt that the hitherto restricted papers would be essential for such a project (McGuire to Fordham, 7 March 1988, CMAC).

CHAPTER FOUR

A new Life of Jung

We come now to the most recent biography of Jung, *Jung: A Biography*, by Deirdre Bair (the title being the same as the English edition of Wehr's biography). This is the longest and most detailed to date. In this chapter, I plan to look at some of the claims made in it, and examine the evidence for them. Given its scale, it deserves to be looked at in more detail than the previous works.

Near the beginning of the book, Bair referred to Jung's attendance during his student days of seances at the home of a figure known only as "Walze".[256] However, this figure turns out to be none other than Jung himself. His lifelong friend, Albert Oeri later recalled, "Carl—or the 'Walze' [roller], as his old friends still call him with the nickname from that time".[257] In reading Bair's book in the light of my researches on Jung, this impression of mistaken identities remained with me throughout.

---

256. Bair, 2003, p. 46.
257. Oeri, 1935, p. 526. A few pages earlier, Bair had actually referred to Oeri's article, (p. 44). In the protocols of the Zofingia society, the student debating organization which Jung attended, his name is generally given as "Jung vulgo Walze" (Staatsarchiv, Basel).

It was only in 1995 that the German *Collected Works*, the preparation of which was supported by the family, was finished, and it was only in 1993 that a complete listing of Jung's manuscripts at the ETH had been prepared. In 1992, the Executive committee of the heirs made a resolution of intent to study Jung's unpublished corpus of manuscripts, seminars, and correspondences, and consider possibilities of further publications.[258] Bair was granted access to the Jung papers in the ETH in accordance with the general conditions of access to all scholars, but was not granted access to materials in the family archives. The executive committee also agreed to answer specific questions. Unfortunately, the answers were not submitted for verification.[259] Bair studied some of Jung's correspondences in the ETH, and was the first biographer to utilize them. Concerning these, she noted that that the card catalogue was restricted, and she had to know which correspondences she wanted to consult.[260] In the main, she did not study the unpublished manuscripts, noting that access had been limited by the Jung estate and the staff at the ETH.[261] Under the conditions of access, the Jung estate cannot restrict access to the manuscripts.

Like Hayman, Bair made use of the *Memories* protocols and the Nameche interviews. Like Brome, she interviewed individuals who knew Jung, and also like Brome, she used anonymous sources. In addition, she also used anonymous private archives. She made more use of materials in public and private archives than previous biographers. Thus, for the general public, Bair's biography presented far more hitherto unknown material than the previous Jung biographies. At the same time, this makes it harder to assess for anyone not familiar with some of these materials.

We pick up the story around the time when Jung entered into communication with Freud. By 1907, Jung had became increasingly disenchanted by the limitations of experimental and statistical

---

258.   Personal communication, Ulrich Hoerni.

259.   Personal communication, Ulrich Hoerni.

260   Bair, 2003, p. xi.

261.   *Ibid.*, p. 830, n. 57. I studied the card catalogue of the correspondences in 1994, and have been working my way through them since then. I also commenced studying the unpublished manuscripts in 1994, and a number of these are discussed in Shamdasani, 2003. A number of other scholars have also studied these.

methods in psychiatry and psychology. In the outpatients clinic at
the Burghölzli, he presented hypnotic demonstrations, which led to
his interest in therapeutics.[262] This led to his interest in therapeutics,
and to the use of the clinical encounter as a method of research.
Jung first met Freud in 1907.[263]

As we have seen, Jung's relationship with Freud has been much
mythologized. It is clear that Freud and Jung came from quite
different intellectual traditions, and were drawn together by shared
interests in the psychogenesis of mental disorders and psychotherapy.[264] Their intention was to form a scientific psychotherapy based
on the new psychology, and in turn, to ground psychology on the
in-depth clinical investigation of individual lives. With the lead of
Bleuler and Jung, the Burghölzli became the centre of the psychoanalytic movement. Due to their advocacy, psychoanalysis gained a
hearing in the German psychiatric world.

From 1909 onwards, Jung embarked on an extensive study of
mythology, comparative religion, anthropology, and folklore. It was
hoped that the application of psychoanalysis would illumine cultural history, which in turn would illumine the psychology of the
individual. He was attempting to construct a phylogenetic biologi-
cally based psychology based on late nineteenth century memory
theories, and a collective transcultural psychology. He supervised
the work of students whom he encouraged to do research on such
topics. One such student was J. J. Honegger.

For Bair, following Richard Noll, what was at issue is the question of whether Jung stole Honegger's work, and consequently, the

262.   Bair claimed that Jung did not practice hypnosis or believe in its
powers (p. 738, n. 84). This is not the case. Volumes 1 to 4 of Jung's *Collected
Works* present numerous cases of hypnosis and discussions of it. For an account
of Jung's involvement with hypnosis, see Shamdasasni, 2001. In 1913, Jung
recalled that he resolved to abandon the use of hypnotic suggestion not because
it was inefficacious, but because he did not understand how it cured: "I was
resolved to abandon suggestion altogether rather than allow myself to be
passively transformed into a miracle-worker" (*CW* 4, § 582).
263.   When Jung visited Freud in March 1909, a loud noise occurred at a
critical point in the conversation, which he interpreted parapsychologically as a
"catalytic exteriorisation phenonemena". For Freud's understanding of this
event, see Freud to Jung, 16 April 1909, (McGuire, 1974, p. 218). Bair mistakenly
stated that this occurred on their first meeting (p. 117).
264.   See Shamdasani, 2003.

idea of the collective unconscious.[265] This is absurd. As I have shown elsewhere, notions of a collective or transindividual unconscious were so widespread in the last quarter of the nineteenth century that it is surprising that actual term, 'collective unconscious,' was not used before Jung as far as I am aware.[266]

Honegger's research work focused on a patient, E. Schwyzer, who was born in 1862. He was a store clerk, and had not had any higher education. He had lived in Paris and London, and, after an attempt at suicide, he was committed to an asylum in London for one and a half years. After this, he went to Zürich, where he was committed to the Burghölzli on 7 October 1901. The case was the subject of Honegger's presentation at the 1910 psychoanalytic congress in Nuremberg. According to Bair, Jung saw something universal in the patient's solar phallus vision in 1901, but there is no evidence to support this dating. I have argued elsewhere that the specific turn which the patient's fantasies took was actually due to the suggestive impact of Honegger's mode of questioning, and that the observation may have followed the inception of the mythological project.[267]

In 1911, Honegger committed suicide. According to Bair, Honegger's papers indicate his "mental illness".[268] I have read through these papers, and do not see what Bair is talking about.[269] As regards contemporaneous indications of Honegger's mental condition we have Jung's comment to Freud that Honegger committed suicide to *avoid* a psychosis,[270] but there is no implication on the part of Jung that Honegger was mentally ill when he

---

265.   Bair, 2003, p. 189.
266.   Shamdasani, 2003, section 3.
267.   Shamdasani, 2003, p. 216.
268.   Bair, 2003, p. 189.
269.   The Honegger papers are in the archives of the ETH in Zurich. A number of years ago, a copy was given to William McGuire for his personal study. McGuire subsequently deposited them in the Library of Congress. The ETH requested the return of their materials. Bair stated that the Jung estate claimed ownership of the papers (2003, p. 642), which is false (personal communication, Ulrich Hoerni).
270.   31 March 1911, McGuire, 1974, p. 412. On 28 June 1911, Jung informed the American psychiatrist Trigant Burrow that Honegger had committed suicide after realizing that he had made the wrong decisions and did not sufficiently believe in life (JP).

was practising as a psychiatrist and working with Jung as a student and assistant. Indeed, in March 1910, when Jung went on a trip to America, he entrusted his patients to Honegger.[271]

Around this time, Jung's theoretical development led to changes in his technique.[272] These changes played an important role in his dispute with Freud. Ernst Falzeder has reconstructed the role played in this by Elfriede Hirschfeld, a patient who was treated by both Freud and Jung. Falzeder noted that "Freud and Jung criticized each other, using the case of Frau Hirschfeld as the ostensible motive".[273] On 2 January 1912, Jung wrote to Freud:

> I said, all she wanted was a little bit of sympathy which you, for very good reasons best known to yourself, may have withheld . . . I myself would not, often very much malgré moi, behave in such an abstract way, because sometimes I couldn't withold my sympathy, and, since it was already there anyway, I gladly offered it to the patient, telling myself that the patient as a human being was entitled to as much esteem and personal concern as the doctor saw fit to grant him.[274]

As Falzeder noted, in retrospect, Freud made the following comments in a paper delivered to his "secret committee" in 1921:

> She was also the first occasion when Jung revealed his doubtful character . . . During a holiday stay in Zurich she once let him come to make his acquaintance. On this occasion he expressed his amazement that she could endure being in analysis with me without warmth and sympathy, and he recommended himself for a treatment in a higher temperature and with more verve.[275]

---

271. Jung to Freud, 9 March 1910, McGuire, 1974, p. 302.
272. On this question, see Jung's discussion of this issue in his 1912 lectures at Fordham University, "Attempt at a portrayal of psychoanalytic theory", CW 4, §§ 407–457. While Jung was in America on this trip, Bair claimed that Emma Jung wrote to him usually every day (2003, p. 229) and noted that the letters are in the Jung family archive (ibid., p. 723, n. 60). However, there are no letters from Emma Jung to C. G. Jung in 1912 there (personal communication, Andreas Jung).
273. Falzeder, 1994, p. 313.
274. McGuire, 1974, pp. 476–477 tr. mod.
275. Cited by Falzeder, 1994, p. 316.

In 1914, in his history of the psychoanalytic movement, Freud cited a letter from a patient of Jung about his analysis with Jung to indicate "the form taken by the Neo-Zurich therapy under these influences":

> This time not a trace of attention was given to the past or the transference. Wherever I thought I recognized the latter it was pronounced to be a pure libidinal symbol. The moral instruction was very fine and I followed it faithfully, but I did not advance a step. It was even more annoying for me than him, but how could I help it? ... Instead of freeing me by analysis, every day brought fresh demands on me, which had to be fulfilled if the neurosis was to be conquered—for instance, inward concentration by means of introversion, religious meditation, resuming life with my wife in loving devotion, etc. It was almost beyond one's strength; it was aiming at a radical transformation of one's whole inner nature. I left the analysis as a poor sinner with intense feelings of contrition and the best resolutions, but at the same time in utter discouragement. Any clergyman would have advised what he recommended, but where was I to find strength?[276]

The aim of Freud's citation was to show that Jung's therapeutic technique had nothing to do with psychoanalysis. The patient in question appears to be none other than Oskar Pfister. In 1914, Karl Abraham wrote to Freud apropos Pfister: "his letter quoted in the 'History' was written in opposition to Jung; with his change of attitude he returns to Jung, and now back to you again!"[277] After reading Freud's work, Jung commented to Poul Bjerre:

> In a breach of medical discretion, Freud has even made hostile use of a patient's letter—a letter which the person concerned, whom I know very well, wrote in a moment of resistance against me. Supposing I were to publish what people have told me about Freud!!!

---

276.   Freud, 1914, pp. 63–64.
277.   16 July 1914, Falzeder, 2002, p. 258. Pfister's vacillations appeared to continue. In 1916, Abraham again wrote to Freud about him, "His letter, which you quoted in the 'History of the Psychoanalytic Movement' was indeed factually correct, but it was written in a period of personal resistance against J., and with his changed attitude all his fine discernment has vanished again" (23 January 1916, *ibid.*, p. 323).

These practices are characteristic of the Viennese policies. Such an enemy is not worth the name.[278]

Despite making use of material from Falzeder's article, Bair claimed that Jung felt that his break with Freud deprived him of the right to use Freud's psychology in his therapy,[279] and that Jung realized that he would have no credibility after Freud's citation of the letter.[280] No sources are given for these claims, which present a misunderstanding of the conflicts between Freud and Jung. There is no indication that his break with Freud *led* Jung to change his practice. Rather, Jung's changes in technique were one source of their conflict.[281]

The outcome of Jung's mythological researches was *Transformation and Symbols of the Libido*. Here, Jung synthesized nineteenth century theories of memory, heredity, and the unconscious and posited a phylogenetic layer to the unconscious that was still present in everyone, consisting of mythological images. Jung attempted to apply his new theory of the libido to explain the symbolism of the mythology and folklore. For Jung, myths were symbols of the libido and they depicted its typical movements. He used the comparative method of anthropology to draw together a vast panoply of myths, and then subjected them to analytic interpretation. He later called this the method of amplification.[282] Jung's work was based on a psychological interpretation of an article written in French by Miss Frank Miller, "Some instances of subconscious creative imagination", which was originally

---

278.   17 July, 1914, Adler, 1975, pp. xxix–xxx.
279.   Bair, 2003, p. 247.
280.   *Ibid.*, p. 246. Bair added that Jung did not respond to Freud's citation of the letter because of his distress and confusion. The letter cited to Bjerre cited above suggests otherwise.
281.   In August 1913, Jung presented a paper in London at the International Medical Congress. Bair erroneously stated that he gave a series of lectures (2003, p. 239). Jung actually gave one lecture, "General aspects of psychoanalysis" (CW 4).
282.   Bair argued that Jung's work began as an attempt to show how myths could be used to explain psychological concepts, which is mistaken (2003, p. 201).The work applied the libido theory to the interpretation of mythological symbols.

published by Theodore Flournoy in his journal, *Archives de Psychologie*.[283]

In the second part of the work, Jung revised and widened the concept of the libido. He noted that while the term stemmed from the sexual sphere, its connotation in psychoanalysis had become much wider. He presented a new model of libido, in which there were three phases of development: a presexual stage, a prepubertal stage starting from around the age of three to five, and maturity. There were a multiplicity of drives and instincts which were distinct from the libido.[284]

Bair claimed that the "terror" of writing the second part of the work led Jung to practise yoga. She noted that for Jung, the second part was in a language that corresponded to how the archetypes spoke, that it embarrassed him and went against the grain, but he was compelled to write it down.[285] No source is given for these statements. In actuality, they stem either from *Memories* or from the protocols, and refer to Jung's subsequent confrontation with the unconscious, and specifically to the composition of the *Black Books*. In *Memories*, Jung stated:

> I was frequently so wrought up that I had to eliminate the emotions through yoga practices. But since it was my purpose to learn what was going on within myself, I would do them only until I had calmed myself and could take up again the work with the unconscious.[286]

Also in *Memories*, when referring to writing down his fantasies in the *Black Books*, Jung stated:

283.   Bair erroneously claimed that Flournoy gave Jung his translation of Frank Miller's fantasies with what he had gleaned from her in conversation and correspondence (2003, p. 213). Frank Miller wrote an article in French, to which Flournoy wrote an introduction. Bair also claimed that Frank Miller actually invented her fantasies (p. 214). There is no evidence to support this. On Frank Miller, see Shamdasani, 1990.

284.   Bair claimed that in the second part of the work, Jung argued that the sex drive did not have primacy, as other factors were present, such as the archetypes of the collective unconscious (2003, p. 201). This is to confound Jung's subsequent theories with his arguments in 1912.

285.   Bair, 2003, p. 224.

286.   Jung/Jaffé, 1962, p. 201, tr. mod. Protocols, LC, p. 145.

First I formulated the things as I had observed them in the "high-flown language," for that corresponds to the style of the archetypes. Archetypes speak the style of high rhetoric, even of bombast. It is a style I find embarrassing; it grates on my nerves . . . but since I did not know what was going on, I had no choice but to write everything down in the style selected by the unconscious itself.[287]

Thus Jung's comments about his experiments in active imagination from 1913 onwards are mistakenly taken to refer to his composition of a scholarly work in 1911–1912.

It was in 1913 that Jung broke of his personal relation with Freud. On 21 September, Freud wrote a letter to Alphonse Maeder in which he indicated that he doubted Jung's 'bona fides'.[288] Maeder communicated this to Jung, who then wrote to Freud indicating that he had resigned his position as the editor of the *Jahrbuch*.[289]

As we have seen, Jung's confrontation with the unconscious has attracted all manner of diagnoses. Like Frank McLynn, Bair referred to Jung's experiences as "psychotic" visions, following the familiar myth of Jung's madness.[290] She did not provide evidence for her diagnosis. In the course of my own study of this period, based on Jung's *Black Books* and his *Red Book*, I have found no evidence which would support such a diagnosis.

In his 1925 seminar, Jung narrated a significant event that occurred when he was writing his fantasies down in the *Black Books*. On one occasion, he wondered what he was doing, and heard a voice which said that it was "art". This led him to think that: "Perhaps my unconscious is forming a personality that is not I, but which is insisting on coming through to expression".[291] He continued his

287. *Ibid.*, p. 202. Protocols, LC, p. 145.
288. Freud archives, LC.
289. 27 October 1913, McGuire, 1974, p. 550. Bair noted that Freud informed Maeder that Jung was an anti-Semite, but the reference given is to Jung's letter to Freud concerning 'bona fides' (p. 240). Freud's letter to Maeder of 21 September 1913 (LC) contains no reference to antisemitism. This may be a confusion with Maeder's statement in his interview with Nameche that he received a letter from Freud in which he wrote, "Maeder, you are an anti-Semite" (CLM, p. 4).
290. Bair, 2003, 290.
291. Jung, 1925, p. 42. In Jung's account here, it seems that this dialogue took place in the autumn of 1913.

dialogues with this figure. He recognized this voice as that of a Dutch woman patient, who had led one of his colleagues to believe that he was a misunderstood artist.[292] I have previously argued that the woman in question—the only Dutch woman in Jung's circle at this time—was Maria Moltzer, and that the colleague in question was Jung's friend and colleague Franz Riklin, who increasingly forsook analysis for painting.[293]

As we have seen, Brome, McLynn, Hayman and others have presented insufficiently substantiated reinterpretations of Jung's "Siegfried" dream in terms of Freud and Sabina Spielrein. In *Memories*, the date of the dream is given as 18 December 1913. Bair commented on this episode, and criticized what she claimed were the liberties that Jaffé took with the protocols. Bair noted that in the protocols, nowhere is the date given, and that there is no account of the panic which would be sufficient for him to contemplate shooting himself, as narrated in *Memories*.[294] By contrast, Bair claimed that Jung credited this dream for bringing his confrontation with the unconscious to a "satisfying conclusion".[295]

What is going on here? On page 98 of the protocols, we find the following comment of Jung's concerning this dream: "I had to shoot myself dead, if I did not understand this dream, I thought at that time".[296] Jung had given Jaffé access to the *Black Books*. If we look at these, we find the date is noted precisely as given by Jaffé:

---

292.   Jung/Jaffé, 1962, *Errinerungen, Träume, Gedanken*, p. 190.

293.   Bair claimed that in the protocols, Jung identified this figure as Maria Moltzer (p. 291). Such an explicit identification is not found in the protocols in the Library of Congress. The argument for Moltzer as the woman in question was made by myself (Shamdasani, 1995, p. 129, 1998a, p. 16). If there exists documentation where Jung explicitly made this identification, it should be produced. In the early 1920s, Riklin painted frescos on the ceilings of Amsthaus 1 in Zürich, together with Augusto Giacometti. Bair misdated this to 1912 (p. 223). On Moltzer, see also Shamdasani, 1998b.

294.   Bair, 2003, p. 727, n. 13.

295.   *Ibid.*, p. 244. The source given for this statement is two unidentified protocols, p. 746, n. 13.

296.   Protocols, *LC*, p. 98. In the protocols, there then follows an excerpt of Jung's discussion of this dream in the 1925 seminar (protocols, pp. 99–100; Jung 1925, pp. 56–57). What Bair cited as Jung's discussion of this dream in the protocols on p. 727, n. 13 is actually a quotation from this excerpt.

18 December 1913.[297] Furthermore, we find there that Jung noted that if he didn't understand the dream, he felt that he should kill himself. Thus, the account in *Memories* accords with Jung's contemporaneous account in the *Black Books*. It also accords with Jung's account of the dream to Bennet, which neither McLynn, Hayman, nor Bair cited, despite the fact that it was published.[298]

It was on 13 December that Jung took the decisive step of commencing to evoke fantasies in a waking state, and to elaborate them. If the Siegfried dream had actually brought his confrontation with the unconscious to a close, the critical phase of it would have only lasted a week—a rather short time for a "descent into the underworld". I have not found any place where Jung states that the dream brought this to a satisfying conclusion, which would be peculiar, as he was just beginning his "confrontation with the unconscious". There is also no suggestion of this in his comments to Bennet, cited earlier.

Throughout 1914, Jung continued with his self-experimentation on a regular basis. He maintained his practice and full professional activity, and in his spare time, he dedicated himself to studying his fantasies, which he wrote in his *Black Books*.[299] Apart from two weeks military service, two weeks in Italy, one week in England and a couple of days in the Engadine, he remained in Zürich in 1914.[300]

Between June and July 1914, Jung had a thrice repeated dream of being in a foreign land and having to return home quickly by ship, followed by the descent of an icy cold.[301] Bair stated that Jung

---

297. Jung, *Black Book* 2, p. 56f, Jung Family archive. Also, when discussing the dream in the 1925 seminar, Jung noted that it occurred "soon after" the fantasy of December 13 (p. 48).

298. See above, p. 40.

299. Bair claimed that Emma Jung was forbidden to read the *Black Books*, and that in early 1914, Toni Wolff was the only person to read them. (pp. 249–250). Material in the Jung family archives suggests otherwise, as will be clear when the *Red Book* is published. Bair also reported that Jung "drew" in the *Black Books*, which was generally not the case.

300. Information from Andreas Jung. Bair erroneously claimed that he was away more than he was at home that year (p. 248).

301. Bair erroneously noted that these dreams contain "yellow flood" and "dark red blood" (2003, p. 243). Neither in *Memories*, nor in the *Black Books* are these motifs to be found.

viewed these dreams as a precognition of the war.[302] However, in Jung's *Black Books*, there is no evidence of this. In actuality, it was only after the outbreak of the war that Jung retrospectively viewed his fantasies as having been precognitive.[303] After this realization, Jung commenced writing the *Red Book*. The outbreak of the war had convinced him that some of his fantasies were precognitive. As he noted in *Memories*, "I had to try to understand what had happened and to what extent my own experience coincided with that of mankind in general".[304]

According to Bair, after his lecture in Aberdeen on 28 July 1914, Jung realized that the only way to form a system distinct from Freud's was to treat himself as a patient. She noted that he recalled the diaries that he had kept until 1900, and that he decided to revive these to embark on observing himself and meditating on the unconscious, "which he would later call individuation".[305] She added that he decided to confine himself to "language metaphors". No source is given for this statement, but it appears to be based on the following statement of Jung to Aniela Jaffé in the protocols:

> This was an attempt to meditate on myself, and [I] began to describe my inner condition. This represented itself to me in a literary metaphor: for example, I was in a cloud, and the sun shone unbearably (sun = consciousness).[306]

This statement actually refers to the commencement of the *Black Books*, which occurred in October 1913. These books do not consist of "random thoughts", "daily happenings", or "jottings from readings", as Bair claimed.[307]

The *Red Book* has not been publically available for study. However, unlike Jung's previous biographers, this did not stop Bair from making a number of striking claims concerning its contents. For example, she noted that in the *Red Book*, Jung presented "illustrated

302. *Ibid.*
303. *Memories*, p. 200; *Analytical Psychology*, p. 44.
304. Jung/Jaffé 1962, p. 200.
305. Bair, 2003, p. 291.
306. Protocols, LC, p. 23. In the margins by this paragraph is written "Black Book".
307. Bair, 2003, p. 291.

drawings of his fantasies accompanied by interpretive texts".[308] However, in the *Red Book*, Jung's drawings generally do not represent his fantasies, nor does he interpret them. The paintings may best be regarded as active imaginations in their own right.

Bair claimed that *Red Book* contains variations of the Salome, Elijah, and Philemon fantasies.[309] This is not the case at all. She went so far as to say that "all" Jung's inner figures stemmed from Goethe's *Faust*.[310] This is not true: a reading of *Memories* is sufficient to disprove this claim, as Jung refers to figures who do not occur in Goethe's *Faust*, such as Ka and Atmavictu (not to mention Elijah and Salome), and the actual text contains many more.

Bair claimed that at this time, Jung abandoned the *Black Books* for the *Red Book*, as he felt that a special book was needed for the language metaphors that arose when Philemon spoke.[311] However, Jung did not abandon the *Black Books*, and he carried on writing in it while he worked on the *Red Book*.

One source on the *Red Book* that Bair cited was Richard Hull. She noted that in 1961 Jung invited Hull to read the *Red Book*, and that Hull considered that it gave "the most convincing proof that Jung's whole system is based on psychotic fantasies" and that it was the work of a lunatic.[312] She added that Jung decided not to publish the *Red Book* "as it lets the cat right out of the bag".[313] The last statement is given in quotes, but its source is unidentified. After viewing the *Red Book*, Hull wrote as follows to William McGuire:

> She [AJ] showed us the famous "Red Book", full of real mad drawings with commentaries in monkish script; I'm not surprised Jung keeps it under lock and key! When he came in and saw it lying—

---

308. *Ibid.*, p. 292.
309. *Ibid.*, p. 292. Bair also stated that the figure of Philemon led Jung to study Gnosticism (p. 396). However, Jung's reading notes (JA) and references in *Transformations and Symbols of the Libido* indicate that he started studying Gnosticism in 1910. Bair reproduced a photograph of Jung's mural of Philemon together with his a mural of a mandala and stated that they are on the wall of his "private room" in his tower at Bollingen (facing p. 370). Actually, they are in separate bedrooms.
310. *Ibid.*, p. 399.
311. *Ibid.*, p. 292.
312. Bair, 2003, p. 293.
313. *Ibid.*, p. 293.

fortunately closed—on the table, he snapped at her: "That should not be here. Take it away!" although she had written me earlier that he had given permission for me to see it.[314]

Thus, it is clear that Hull made no prolonged study of the work. In my own experience, it took several years of study to understand the work properly, and it was not until I studied the *Black Books* that I fully understood it.

While the *Red Book* has not yet been published, one critical text from this period has been published. In 1916, Jung composed a work which he titled "The seven sermons to the dead". In *Memories*, Jung noted that "these conversations with the dead formed a kind of prelude to what I had to communicate to the world about the unconscious: a kind of pattern of order and interpretation of its general contents".[315] The text presents an outline of a psychocosmology written in a literary and symbolic style. Bair stated that it is like a self-help textbook, which is a bizarre description.[316] According to Bair, the *Sermones* spontaneously arose from nowhere.[317] In actual fact, the *Sermones* presented a preliminary synthesis of the points that Jung had been slowly working towards in the *Black Books* and in the *Red Book*. In *Memories*, Jung gave the following account of the circumstances in which it arose:

> Around five o'clock in the afternoon on Sunday the front-door bell began to ring frantically. It was a bright summer; the two maids were in the kitchen, from which the open square outside the front door could be seen. Everyone immediately looked to see who was there, but there was no one in sight. I was sitting near the door bell, and not heard but saw it moving. We all simply stared at one another. The atmosphere was thick, believe me! Then I knew that something had to happen. The whole house was filled as if there

---

314.   Hull to McGuire, 17 March 1961, BA.

315.   Jung/Jaffé, 1962, p. 217.

316.   Bair, 2003, p. 297. Bair claimed that the *Sermones* followed the style and subject matter of the works of G. R. S Mead, and that Jung was studying sixteen or eighteen volumes of Mead's work at this time (p. 296). The first statement is mistaken. No source is given for the second, and no evidence exists to support it.

317.   *Ibid.*, p. 290.

were a crowd present, crammed full of spirits. They were packed deep right up to the door, and the air was so thick it was scarcely possible to breathe. As for myself, I was all a-quiver with the question: "For God's sake, what in the world is this?" Then they cried out in chorus "We have come back from Jerusalem where we found not what we sought." That is the beginning of the *Septem Sermones*.[318]

According to Bair, this event occurred on a stifling day in the summer of 1916.[319] She recounted how Toni Wolff had left after eating a meal with the family and spending the afternoon with Jung by the lake. She added that a thunderstorm loomed, and that everyone hoped that it would end the uncomfortable heat.[320] The narrative sounds almost like an eyewitness account. Bair stated that her account is based on two "protocols", which are unidentified.[321] If one consults the *Black Books*, one sees that the day in question was actually 30 January 1916.[322] Heatwaves are not exactly common in Zürich in the winters.

After completing the work, Jung had it privately printed. Through the years, he gave many copies to students, friends and colleagues. Bair claimed that when Jung recopied the text, he was horrified by what he read, and decided to let few people read it.[323] No sources are given for this comment. Jung's "horror" would be very strange, given that the *Sermones* presented the elaboration of what he had been working on for several years, and would continue to elaborate, and moreover, given that he regarded it as "a kind of prelude to what I had to communicate to the world about the unconscious".[324] In 1925, the work was translated by H. G. Baynes, and privately published by Watkins Books. Jung gave copies of these to his English-language students. As a number of commentators have correctly pointed out, the *Sermones* presents the

---

318. Jung/Jaffé 1962, pp. 215–216.
319. Bair, 2003, p. 293.
320. *Ibid*.
321. *Ibid*., p. 746, n. 13.
322. Jung, *Black Book 5*, p. 190, Jung family archives.
323. Bair, 2003, p. 295.
324. Jung/Jaffé, 1962, p. 217.

first account of many important themes which would preoccupy Jung throughout his later work.[325]

At this point in time, Bair claimed that Jung abandoned the *Red Book*, as well as the figure of Philemon, as he realized that he could not publicly show the raw material of the *Sermones*.[326] In actual fact, he continued to work on the *Red Book* for over a decade longer, and continued to deliberate concerning whether to publish it. It was only around 1930 that he put it to one side. Bair noted that the composition of the *Red Book* and the *Sermones* served two important functions: they dispelled the ghosts that haunted his house and provided domestic harmony, and brought about the end of his concentration on his personal unconscious.[327] In Jung's own understanding, his confrontation with the unconscious did not signify a concentration on his personal unconscious, but rather, marked the exploration of the collective unconscious. And this endeavour by no means ended in 1916. In his postscript to the *Red Book*, Jung wrote:

> I worked on this book for 16 years. The acquaintance with alchemy in 1930 took me away from it. The beginning of the end came in 1928, when Wilhelm sent me the text of the "Golden Flower", this alchemical treatise. There the contents of this book found their way into reality. I could work on it no longer.

> It will seem to a superficial observer like an insanity. It could also have become one, if I had not been able to hold the overwhelming force of the original experience. I always knew, that that experience contained valuable things, and because of this I knew not better than to write it in a "valuable", that is, expensive book, and to paint it with the images that appeared.[328]

As noted, the *Red Book* forms the centre of Jung's later work. If one does not get this right, it has serious cumulative consequences. If one does not place Jung's confrontation with the unconscious in a proper perspective, or understand the significance of the *Red Book*,

325.   The *Septem Sermones* was published as an appendix to the German edition of *Memories*, and added to the later American editions. See especially Christine Maillard, 1993, and Alfred Ribi, 1999, pp. 132–257.

326.   Bair, 2003, p. 295.

327.   *Ibid.*, p. 297.

328.   Jung/Jaffé, *Errinnerungen, Traume, Gedanken*, 1962, p. 387.

one is in no place to understand fully Jung's intellectual development from 1913 onwards, and not only that, but his life as well: for
it was his inner life which dictated his movements in the world. If
a work does not present an accurate account of Jung's prime
concerns in the teens and the 1920s, it is not well positioned to show
how Jung's concerns in the 1930s, 1940s, and 1950s directly grew
out of this. For Jung's work on his fantasies in *Black Books* and the
Red Book formed the core of his later work, as he himself contended.
The *Red Book* is at the centre of Jung's life and work. A *definitive*
biography of Jung without an accurate account of it would be like
writing the life of Dante without the *Commedia*, or Goethe without
Faust.

We have seen some indications of the shortcomings of how
Bair's biography deals with Jung's inner life. How does it fare with
the social organization of analytical psychology, and Jung's relations with his followers? We may address this question by looking
at its treatment of the Psychological Club.

This was founded at the beginning of 1916 in Zürich, through a
gift of 360,000 Swiss francs from Edith Rockefeller McCormick. It
was initially housed in a sumptuous property on Löwenstrasse 1.
At its inception, it had approximately sixty members. For Jung, the
aim of the Club was to study the relation of individuals to the
group, and to provide a naturalistic setting for psychological observation to overcome the limitations of one to one analysis, and to
provide a venue where patients could learn to adapt to social situations. At the same time, a professional body of analysts continued
to meet together as the Association for Analytical Psychology.[329]

The Club was underused, and there was little participation from
the members. This led to protracted discussions concerning the
"Club problem", in which members attempted to come to an agreement as to the value and purpose of the Club. Bair claimed that on
13 November 1916, a paper was read to the Club by Harold
McCormick on the subject of the Club problem.[330] However, an
examination of the minutes of the Psychological Club indicate that
no such event took place. In actuality, a letter was sent to members

---

329. On the formation of the Psychological Club, see Shamdasani (1998a).
330. Bair, 2003, p. 274.

of the Club by Emma Jung, soliciting their views on the Club problem.[331] The copy of McCormick's work in the McCormick archives has the following noted by hand: "To the executive committee of the Psychology Club, Frau Dr. Carl Jung—President, By Request. Respectfully submitted, Harold F. McCormick, November 13, 1916".[332] Thus, it was actually his reply to Emma Jung's circular. Bair claimed that most of the members directed their replies to Harold McCormick's paper and noted that Moltzer "disdainfully" called it a letter.[333] This is not the case, as many of the replies make no mention of McCormick's reply. As noted, it was not a paper delivered to the Club, so Moltzer's description is not inappropriate.

In a previous work, I studied in detail an unsigned text, which had been the basis of Richard Noll's claims that under the guise of forming a psychological science, Jung had formed a new religion based on his self-deification as the Aryan Christ. The text, which I call "analytical collectivity", outlines out a model for the psychological development of the individual, through undergoing and overcoming the experience of deification, and develops parallels between this and Christ's crucifixion. It ends with sketching out how individuals experiencing this could come together to form an analytical collectivity, which the author claims was prophetically anticipated by Goethe in his poem "The Mysteries". For this reason, the author approves of the Psychological Club, and sees it as a vehicle for embodying such an analytical collectivity. Noll had claimed that the text was by Jung, that it was presented by him at the inaugural meeting of the Psychological Club, which took place on 26 February 1916, and that it presented the esoteric messianic mission of the Jung Cult.[334] I demonstrated that no such text was presented at the inaugural meeting, and that there was sufficient evidence to demonstrate that Jung was not the author of the text, and that the most likely author was Maria Moltzer.[335]

---

331.   Bair claimed that the only member of the Club who declined was Fanny Bowditch Katz. In actuality, between half and two-thirds of the membership responded.

332.   McCormick papers, State Historical Society of Wisconsin, Madison.

333.   Bair, 2003, p. 276.

334.   Noll, 1994, 1997.

335.   I wrote: "these points strongly suggest that 'Analytical collectivity' was actually written by Moltzer. Whilst this is not definitively proved, the

Bair criticized my work and defended Noll's scholarship, and argued that each of our cases for authorship should be taken as unproven. She put forward the case that Franz Riklin should be considered as another candidate, and suggested that both Riklin and Moltzer may have been responsible for the content of the text, and that some of the handwriting on the text resembled that of Riklin. Another possibility she suggested is that Riklin wrote these comments on Jung's draft, or that he was the author.[336]

The question of considering Riklin as a candidate for the authorship of the text is certainly a valid one. However, I actually considered this and discarded it during the course of my research for my previous book. I closely studied examples of Riklin's handwriting, and found that they bear no resemblance to the writing on the text in the Countway library.[337] More critically, Riklin wrote a reply to the Club inquiry, dated 16 November, 1916. He stated that his few visits to the Club had convinced him that there was a spirit there that was no good for him, and it presented nothing in common with his life and needs. He couldn't identify the Club with analysis, and found that many were against him, which he considered went beyond what he considered tolerable human relations. He noted that he would have put up with what he had experienced towards him if he had the sense that he was needed, but he had other tasks. He ended by turning the question around, and asking, what did the Club want from him, or what did it want to criticize? So far, he had heard little that was useful.[338] I find it quite inconceivable that the same person who wrote the above would also have written the visionary manifesto for the Club embodied in "analytical collectivity". Thus, the most likely author still remains Maria Moltzer.[339]

---

balance of the evidence clearly points in this direction" (Shamdasani, 1998a, p. 72). "We have seen that no positive corroborative evidence has arisen to indicate that 'Analytical collectivity' was by Jung, and that sufficient evidence exists to refute the claim that Jung was the author, beyond all reasonable doubt" (p. 84).

336.   Bair, 2003, p. 741, n. 17 and 18.

337.   I am happy to supply a PDF file of the relevant scripts to anyone interested.

338.   Archives, Psychological Club, Zürich. Riklin made no reference to Harold McCormick's letter.

339.   Moltzer resigned from the Club in 1918. Bair claimed that she subsequently returned to Holland for the rest of her life (p. 259). She actually

If there are shortcomings in how Bair's biography deals with Jung's inner life and the social organization of analytical psychology, how does it deal with his outer life? To explore this question, we may consider how the biography treats Jung's travels.

In the 1920s, Jung embarked upon a series of travels, to North Africa (1920), to New Mexico (1924–1925), and to Kenya and Uganda (1925). These travels formed part of Jung's attempt to forge a psychology that had cross-cultural validity. Furthermore, given Jung's theses concerning phylogenetic inheritance, it followed that what one could witness in less civilized cultures could correspond in some manner to phylogenetic layers in the unconscious of Europeans. For Jung, such travels could be considered as a form of phylogenetic time travelling. Thus, the motivation for his travels directly stemmed from the theoretical issues with which he was engaged.

At the end of 1924, Jung visited New Mexico. Bair claimed that the ethnologist and linguist Jaime de Angulo had maintained that the Pueblos were "too civilised" and did not deserve serious study.[340] The opposite was actually the case. On 16 January 1925, Jaime de Angulo had expressed his intentions to Mabel Dodge:

> I made up my mind that I would kidnap him if necessary and take him to Taos. It was quite a fight because his time was so limited, but I finally carried it. And he was not sorry that he went. It was a revelation to him, the whole thing. Of course I had prepared Mountain Lake. He and Jung made contact immediately and had a long talk on religion. Jung said that I was perfectly right in all that I had intuited about their psychological condition. He said that evening "I had the extraordinary sensation that I was talking to an Egyptian priest of the fifteenth century before Christ".[341]

According to Bair, what Mountain Lake told Jung was superficial.[342] In actuality, Jung considered this one of the key conversations in his life. To Cary de Angulo, he wrote that: "I made friends with

---

remained in Switzerland, and lived at 198 Zollikerstrasse, Zollikerberg. She was buried in Zollikon cemetery.

340. Bair, 2003, p. 335.
341. 16 January 1925, Dodge Papers, BL.
342. Bair, 2003, p. 336.

Mountain Lake and I talked to him sympathetically as if he were a patient in advanced analysis, it was a great time".[343] According to Bair, what Jung had to say about his time in Taos boiled down to just a few paragraphs in the *Memories* protocols in which he appeared to be irritated to have to talk about it.[344] In actuality, Jung dealt with his experiences in Taos at length in a manuscript entitled "African Voyage".[345]

That same year, Jung visited the Wembley Exhibition in London, where he was impressed by the survey of tribes under British rule. He consequently decided to make a trip to Africa.[346] Jung made the trip together H. G. Baynes and George Beckwith. Along the way, they met an English woman called Ruth Bailey, who then joined them for the rest of the trip. The trip made a profound impression on Jung. On the way back, they followed the course of the Nile up north. Jung subsequently recalled:

> Thus the journey from the heart of Africa to Egypt became, for me, a kind of drama of the birth of light. That drama was intimately connected with me, with my psychology ... I had not known in advance what Africa would give me; but here lay the satisfying answer, the fulfilling experience. It was worth more than any ethnological yield would have been ... I had wanted to find out how Africa would affect me, and I had found out.[347]

By contrast, Bair viewed Jung's travels as a form of escapism.[348] She noted that Jung's trip to East Africa enabled him to reflect on what in his "home 'atmosphere'" was "too highly charged to endure".[349] The implication is that Jung travelled to get away from

343. 19 January 1925, BP.
344. Bair, 2003, p. 337.
345. Bair stated that the account in *Memories* was evidently pieced together from what Jung said about Taos in various passages in the *Collected Works* (p. 762, n. 40). Actually, it was excerpted from the manuscript, "African Voyage". It is explicitly stated in *Memories* that the section is an "extract from an unpublished manuscript" (1962, p. 274). On this ms., see Shamdasani, 2003, pp. 323–328.
346. Jung/Jaffé, 1962, p. 282.
347. Jung/Jaffé, 1962, pp. 303–304.
348. Bair, 2003, p. 357.
349. *Ibid.*, p. 340.

the triangular situation between himself, his wife, and Toni Wolff. The sentence cited actually comes from *Memories*, and Jung was not referring to his "home" but to Europe in general: "the atmosphere had become too highly charged for me in Europe".[350] Bair claimed that on Jung's return, he wondered why he went.[351] No source is given for this statement, and it is contradicted by the abiding sense of the significance of his trip which is present in *Memories*.[352] According to Bair, Jung reconsidered the papers and talks he had been producing and asked himself whether they contained a coherent message.[353] No source is given for this statement. In actuality, on Jung's return, he continued to work on the *Red Book*, and there are no signs that he was in any doubt that it contained a coherent message. Bair then referred to the following statement from the *Memories* protocols, without noting where they are from:

> My "scientific" question went: what would happen if I switched off consciousnessness? I noticed from dreams that something stood in the background, and I wanted to give this a fair chance to come forward.[354]

She also referred to Jung's comments about resorting to yoga, which she had previously referred to in connection with the composition of the second half of *Transformations and Symbols of the Libido*.[355] In actuality, these passages do not refer to Jung's thoughts and activities after his African voyage, but to his confrontation with the unconscious, and more specifically, to the years between 1913 and 1917.[356] There is no evidence that Jung continued to practise

---

350.   Jung/Jaffé 1962, p. 303. The sentence in German actually reads: "That the air had become too thick for me in Europe."

351.   Bair, 2003, p. 357.

352.   Bair claimed that the Psychological Club wanted a further seminar based on Jung's experiences (2003, p. 357). Such a request was not noted in the Club minutes. Bair also claimed that Jung received requests for new writings and translations "every day" (*ibid.*). I have made a comprehensive study of Jung's correspondences in the 1920s, and this is simply not the case.

353.   Bair, 2003, p. 357.

354.   Protocols, LC, p. 381.

355.   Bair, 2003, p. 357. See above, p. 94.

356.   After his Africa trip, Bair referred to Jung's annual month of military service (pp. 361–362). However, after the First World War, Jung was only on

yoga after this period. Chronology is the foundation of historical work. Without an accurate chronology, a biography lacks a firm basis.

As we have seen, it was in 1928 that Jung's work on the *Red Book* began to draw to a close, when the Sinologist Richard Wilhelm sent him a copy of the Chinese text, *The Secret of the Golden Flower*. Jung's collaborations with Orientalists such as Wilhelm, Heinrich Zimmer, Walter Evans-Wentz, and Wilhelm Hauer played an important role in his attempt to construct a psychology which had both historical and cross-cultural validity. According to Bair, *The Secret of the Golden Flower* gave Jung the courage to make public his study of alchemy, which he been keeping "almost sheepishly hidden".[357] She added that this enabled him to overcome Toni Wolff's objections that alchemy was simply quackery. Jung himself had this to say about the significance of the text for him in his preface to the second German edition of 1938:

> My deceased friend, Richard Wilhelm ... sent me the text of *The Secret of the Golden Flower* at a time that was crucial for my own work. This was in 1928. I had been investigating the processes of the collective unconscious since the year 1913, and had obtained results that seemed to me questionable in more than one respect... My results, based on fifteen years of effort, seemed inconclusive, because no possibility of comparison offered itself.... The text that Wilhelm sent me helped me out of this difficulty. It contained exactly those items I had long sought for in vain among the Gnostics. Thus the text afforded me a welcome opportunity to publish, at least in a provisional form, some of the essential results of my investigations.

---

military service twice—for five days in 1923 and 1927 (personal communication, Andreas Jung).

357.   Bair, 2003, p. 395. Concerning Jung's religious attitudes, Bair stated that Jung once described himself as a "Christian-minded agnostic" (p. 127). The phrase comes from a letter Jung which wrote to Eugene Rolfe on 19 November 1960, in response to Rolfe's book, *The Intelligent Agnostic's Introduction to Christianity*. Jung wrote: "you have fulfilled your task of demonstrating the approach to Christianity to a Christian-minded agnostic" (Adler, 1975, p. 610). The phrase is not a self-description, but refers to the intended reader of Rolfe's book. On Rolfe's correspondence with Jung concerning his book, see Rolfe, 1989, p. 130f.

At that time it seemed to me a matter of no importance that *The Secret of the Golden Flower* is not only a Taoist text concerned with Chinese yoga, but is also an alchemical treatise. A deeper study of the Latin treatises has taught me better and has shown me that the alchemical character of the text is of prime significance.[358]

Thus, Jung here notes that he did not initially realize the significance of the alchemical nature of the text, and in fact, he does not refer to alchemy in his commentary to the text![359]

Concerning Toni Wolff's relation to alchemy, it is interesting to note that Thadeus Reichstein, who subsequently won the Nobel prize for Chemistry, presented a paper on the subject to the Psychological Club on 7 Nov 1931. He commenced by saying that the president of the Club had invited him to lecture on alchemy a year ago. The president of the Club was Toni Wolff.[360] In 1946, she presented a paper to the Analytical Psychology Club in London, which was taken up with explaining and justifying why Jung took up alchemy, and indicating the significance of its study.[361]

Another Orientalist with whom Jung collaborated with was the Indologist Wilhelm Hauer, who also founded the German Faith Movement. Bair stated that Jung had practised yoga for twenty years, and was interested in Hauer's views concerning its utility in psychotherapy.[362] However, there is no evidence that Jung practised yoga for twenty years: he frequently cautioned Westerner's against its use, and his correspondence with Hauer shows no signs of a

358.   Jung, CW 13, pp. 3–4.
359.   Bair claimed that the first results of Jung's research into alchemy was *The Psychology of the Transference* in 1946 (p. 526). This was actually preceded by "Dream symbols of the individuation process" (1936), "The process of redemption in alchemy" (1937), "Some remarks on the visions of Zosimos" (1938), "The spirit Mercurius" (1943), *Psychology and Alchemy* (1944), "The enigma of Bologna" (1945) and "The philosophical tree" (1945).
360.   "Ueber Alchemie", Library of the Psychological Club, Zürich. Reichstein later won the Nobel prize for Chemistry.
361.   Toni Wolff, (1946). A similar point is made by Hayman, who cites this article (1999, p. 288). We may also note that Toni Wolff's paper, "Christianity within," took its point of departure from Jung's *Psychology and Alchemy* (in Wolff, 1959).
362.   Bair, 2003, p. 434. On Jung's collaboration with Hauer, see my introduction to Jung, 1932.

practical interest in yoga.[363] What interested Jung was the *symbolism* of yoga, and the parallels between this and the individuation processes of his patients. Bair stated that in 1934, Jung severed all connection to Hauer.[364] This is not the case, as their correspondence, which continues through to 1938, shows that they maintained amicable colleagiate terms, and discussed the possibility of several collaborative projects.[365] Indeed, Hauer presented a series of lectures to the Psychological Club in 1938, which Bair noted later on, which contradicts the previous statements.[366]

Jung's interdisciplinary relations with such scholars featured prominently in his speech at the founding of the Jung Institute in 1948, where he presented a list of about twenty topics for further research in complex psychology.[367] According to Bair, this list actually represented the topics which Jung focused on for the rest of his life and that he completed research on them. A study of his subsequent works shows that neither is the case. As was clearly indicated, the list represented Jung's recommendations for students.[368]

Finally, we come to the issue of sex.[369]

> Jung to Spielrein: When I fall in love, one of my first instincts is to feel sorry for the woman involved, because I know, whatever she may imagine when the affair starts, what she really wants is something permanent, the everlasting peace of the double bed, something resolved.[370]

This statement occurs in Christopher Hampton's recent play, *The Talking Cure*. There is no evidence that it—or anything like it—ever

---

363. Jung, "Yoga and the West" (1936). CW 11.
364. Bair, 2003, p. 434.
365. JA.
366. Bair, 2003, p. 469. This is an example of what Richard Ellmann referred to in his review of Bair's Beckett biography as the way in which Bair "hangs on to wrong views even while amassing information that discredits them" (Ellmann, 1978, p. 236).
367. Bair, 2003, p 750, n. 36. Bair noted that Jung abandoned this term and referred to his work as "analytical psychology". The reverse is actually the case.
368. *Ibid.*, p. 534. On this topic, see Shamdasani, 2003, pp. 345–347.
369. Justin Kaplan noted: "By current standards, biographies without voyeuristic, erotic thrills are like ballpark hot dogs without mustard" (1994, p. 1).
370. Hampton 2002, p. 50.

took place. As we have seen, much speculation and rumour has surrounded Jung's relations with his female patients, and has been taken as established fact.

A former editor of the *Journal of Analytical Psychology*, Coline Covington, asserted that:

> Soon after his treatment of Sabina [Spielrein], Jung suffered from what seems to have been a psychotic breakdown. Following this episode, Jung continued to exhibit compelling erotic transferences to his women patients (to the point of including Toni Wolff in his domestic household) in which he would replicate his childhood relationships—his intense relationship with his nurse and more distant one with his mother and his desire to eliminate his father altogether so as not to have to know about his own need for a father who would both love him and his mother.[371]

The implication of this is that Jung's treatment and relation with Spielrein played a role in his "psychotic breakdown". However, Jung's formal treatment of Spielrein actually took place in 1905. Covington does not cite which patients she is referring to, or any evidence to show that Jung had "compelling erotic transferences" to them, but she somehow "knows" what Jung didn't know, namely that in these relations, Jung was unconsciously replicating his unavowed Oedipal desires.[372]

One case which has attracted speculation is that of Christiana Morgan. In the 1930s, Jung presented a series of seminars to the Psychological Club on her visions. At the beginning of his seminar, he indicated his intention:

> the lectures are about the development . . . of the transcendent function out of dreams and visions, and the actual representing of those images which ultimately serve in the synthesis of the individual: the reconciliation of the pairs of opposites and the whole process of individuation.[373]

---

371. Covington, 2001, p. 114.

372. There has been a great deal of mythology written concerning Sabina Spielrien and Jung's relation with her. For correctives, see Angela Graf-Nold (2001), Zvi Lothane (1999), and Fernando Vidal (2001).

373. Jung, 1930–1934, p. 3. Bair suggested that the reason why Jung may have chosen to discuss Morgan's work was because it would offer an opportunity

Christiana Morgan has been the subject of a biography by Claire Douglas. In this, Douglas contended that Jung exploited Morgan, and entered into a sexual relationship with her. Douglas stated that after Morgan's death, Henry Murray sent her correspondence with Jung to Gerhard Adler, who forwarded them to Franz Jung. She commented:

> Until the Jung family releases the documents they own, there can only be suppositions about J's problems with his anima and with countertransference, and about that gossip that Jung broke through a number of his patients' rings of fire by sexually exploiting them.[374]

Bair in turn cited and affirmed this position. She stated that the Jung estate claims that the letters exist, but, up to 2003, has not made them available to scholars.[375]

Living members of the Jung heirs do not know of such a hidden cache of documents.[376] There are a number of letters between Jung and Christiana Morgan at the Jung archives at the ETH, which are accessible. I consulted these in 2002. They do not provide any evidence of sexual exploitation on the part of Jung, and do not support the account of their relationship presented by Douglas and Bair. I also found no evidence for this in the papers of Christiana Morgan at the Countway Library of Medicine at Harvard, nor in the Henry Murray Papers in the Houghton Library at Harvard. If individuals wish to make such claims, then they are beholden to provide the evidence for them. On 31 October 1930, Jung wrote to Morgan:

> This letter is a humble request—would you give me the permission, to use your material you trusted to my hands, in order to explain the secrets of unconscious initiation processes? As a matter of fact

---

for triangular relations between the participants to be worked out on a neutral terrain, which is quite implausible. She claimed that the lectures parallelled Jung's "strong attraction" towards Morgan, but does not provide sufficient evidence for this (Bair, 2003, p. 391).

374.   Douglas 1993, p. 167. There is no indication of an affair between Jung and Morgan in Forrest Robinson's biography of Henry Murray (1992), which is based on extensive interviews with Murray.

375.   Bair, 2003, p. 777, n. 67.

376.   Personal communication, Ulrich Hoerni.

I already used it in a course of 12 German doctors, from a purely impersonal point of view naturally, hiding any personal inferences.[377]

While the seminars were in progress, Jung sent Morgan copies of the notes which were prepared. In June 1931, Morgan thanked Jung for not having detracted from the quality of the visions, and for actually having enhanced them.[378] During the course of the seminars, there was some gossip about the identity of the subject. On 5 November 1931, Morgan wrote to Jung that she had considered this in advance, and felt all right about it. She was not pleased that Peter Baynes had informed someone as to her identity, but ultimately had a sense that such experiences were not purely personal and belong to Jung and his work as much as to herself.[379] In a later letter on 15 August 1932, Jung explained the attitude he took to her material:

> Concerning the trances I am well aware of the personal side of it, but I carefully kept away from any hint to the personal implications. Otherwise people begin to find it too interesting and then they fall into the error to devour each others personal psychology instead of looking for themselves and learning the more difficult task of an impersonal attitude. There are some, quick enough to grasp something of the actual personal background and it is often difficult to keep them off the scent. Life on a personal level is the smaller affair, the higher level however is impersonal. And there is such a thing as responsibility to history.[380]

Many years later, Morgan wrote to Jung informing him of the gratitude in which she and Henry Murray held him. She informed him that it was through him, and in particular, his concept of the anima, that they found the "Way", and that they owed their creative life and joy to him.[381]

---

377. JA, orig. in English.
378. *Ibid.*
379. Bair erroneously stated that there was no such gossip during the course of the seminars, while also claiming that Jung betrayed Morgan's privacy, as she could be recognized (2003, p. 391).
380. JA, orig. in English.
381. 8 June 1948, JA.

In a similar manner to Brome, Bair utilized anonymous sources. Also like Brome, these sources are mentioned in connection to comments about Jung's alleged extra-marital relationships. Bair noted that around 1907 "As the women fluttered before him, his numerous flirtations grew increasingly dangerous, and by extension, increasingly exciting".[382] No source is given for this statement. Referring to events in 1909, she argued that diaries of some wealthy women who lived in Zürichberg hinted at other liaisons, and that there is one in which a woman graphically described "treatment sessions" in her house which turned into sex.[383] This is a serious allegation. It goes beyond Brome's claims concerning Jung's extra-marital relations, as it alleges that these encounters took place in a context of treatment, and hence would have constituted malpractice. In the footnote, Bair noted that in her interviews with daughters of these women, they indicated that "something between flirtation and actual affairs" had occurred between their mothers and Jung.[384] We are not told how many women these were. In historical work, it is essential to provide evidence for one's assertions. Otherwise, there is no way to judge their veracity. I have studied a number of diaries of patients of Jung. In my own experience, in some of these it is not always easy to differentiate reported events and conversations from dreams, active imaginations, or fantasies.

In addition to anonymous sources, there are quite a number of statements for which no sources are given. An example is the following: speaking of Jung's financial circumstances in 1914, Bair referred to "Jung's insistence that he was incapable of adult activity".[385] Where does such a strange statement come from?

The relationships that Brome and Bair allege may have taken place: but firm evidence needs to be given for them. Given the errors in their works, I will, for the time being, give little credence to such allegations until documents are presented in the public domain. The same goes for other information attributed to anonymous sources, unidentified private archives, and to unattributed information.

---

382. Bair, 2003, p. 114.
383. Ibid., p. 181.
384. Ibid., p. 708, n. 46.
385. Ibid., p. 253.

This chapter has by no means been a comprehensive review of Bair's biography, and has focused on factual errors, of which there are many more than those detailed above.[386] As a result of the cumulative effect of these errors, I find the general portrait of Jung in this biography to be quite unconvincing. If, as Jung had maintained, the cardinal task for any biography of him was to put the development of his thought in the centre, the latest biography does not succeed, any more than those before it.

---

386.   On Bair's errors in her treatment of Jung's relationship to Victor White, see Ann Lammers, 2004.

Conclusion: life after biography?

We began by considering Jung's reservations about his suitability as a subject for a biography. In retrospect, it appears that his qualms were well placed, and indeed, could even be considered to be prophetic of the fate which was to befall him. On the basis of the foregoing, I submit that none of the biographies of Jung to date can be regarded as definitive, and that they all leave something to be desired. The multiple lives of Jung since his death have not brought us significantly closer to the historical Jung, and the first, by Barbara Hannah, is, in my view, the most reliable and most important.

We have seen that the "lives" of Jung after his death have provided a variegated series of portraits. At times it can be hard to recognize the subject of one as being the same as the subject of another. This work has attempted to assess them in terms of their documentary evidence, their use of published and unpublished sources, and the coherence of their arguments. The following are some of the shortcomings we have seen in some of them: chronological confusions, failures to consult all pertinent published materials, misreadings of materials in the public domain and in archives, reliance on anonymous sources, interprefactions, repetition of myths, insufficient grasp of Jung's ideas and their historical context, and insufficient consultation of Jung's own manuscripts and correspondences. We have also seen how Jung's dreams and fantasies, all too often, have functioned like Rorschach inkblots, and attracted all manner of fantasies, and that the boundary line between novels and plays about Jung and non-fictional works has not always been as sharp as it could be.

What, then, are the prospects for future biographies of Jung? These shortcomings may actually be corrected in a straightforward way, through the use of contemporary historical methods.[387] As some have noted, it goes without saying that a definitive biography of Jung would only be possible once all the key sources are made available and studied. The publication of his unpublished manuscripts, correspondences, and seminars in scholarly historical editions, will enable future biographies, indeed, all future studies of Jung, to be better grounded in the primary texts. After the publication of Jung's *Red Book*, future biographies may finally start to be based on the most important primary material. At the same time, it is important to stress that biography cannot take the place of historical contextualization.

If this survey of half a century of attempts to write Jung's life has shown that they have left a lot to be desired, this conclusion simultaneously underscores the fact that a great deal of primary research by many hands remains to be done. Such research has the potential to transform currently received opinions about Jung to an extent which is hard to envisage.

---

387.   For exemplars of biographical works that do full justice to social and intellectual contexts, see Janet Browne's biography of Darwin (1995, 2002), Lawrence Friedman's of Erikson (1999), and Fernando Vidal's of Piaget (1994). A fuller consideration of these works would lead one to distinguish between two distinct genres: biography by professional biographers, which has been the main consideration of this book, and biography by historians of science. It is also important to point out that alongside the Jung biographical tradition, important historical research on Jung by many scholars has been quietly going on.

REFERENCES

Adler, G. (Ed.) (1973). *C. G. Jung Letters, Volume 1: 1906–1950*, in with Aniela Jaffé, R. F. C. Hull (Trans.). Bollingen Series, Princeton: Princeton University Press and London: Routledge.

Adler, G. (Ed.) (1975). *C. G. Jung Letters, Volume 2: 1951–1961*, in with Aniela Jaffé, R. F. C. Hull (Trans.). Bollingen Series, Princeton: Princeton University Press and London: Routledge.

Baynes, H. G. (1940). *Mythology of the Soul: A Research into the Unconscious from Schizophrenic Dreams and Paintings*. London: Baillière & Co.

Bair, D. (2003). *Jung: A Biography*. New York: Little Brown.

Bennet, E. A. (1961). *C. G. Jung*. London: Barrie and Rockliff.

Bennet, E. A. (1966). *What Jung really Said*. London: Macdonald.

Bennet, E. A. (1982). *Meetings with Jung: Conversations recorded by E. A. Bennet During the Years 1946–1961*, London.

Bishop, P. (1998). On the history of analytical psychology: C. G. Jung and Rascher Verlag: Part 2. *Seminar*, 34: 354–387.

Borch-Jacobsen, M., & Shamdasani, S. (2001). Une visite aux archives Freud. *Ethnopsy: Les mondes contemporains de la guérison*, 3: 141–188.

Borch-Jacobsen, M., & Shamdasani, S. (forthcoming). *The Freud Report: An Inquiry into the History of Psychoanalysis*.

Brome, V. (1978). *Jung: Man and Myth*. London: MacMillan.

Browne, J. (1995). *Charles Darwin Vol. 1, Voyaging*. London: Jonathan Cape.

Browne, J. (2002). *Charles Darwin Vol. 2., The Power of Place*. London: Jonathan Cape.

Claudel, P. (1954). *Mémoires improvisés*. Paris: Gallimard.

Covington, C. (2001). Comment on the Burghölzli hospital records of Sabina Spielrein. *Journal of Analytical Psychology*, 46(1): 105–116.

Douglas, C. (1993). *Translate this Darkness: The Life of Christiana Morgan, the Veiled Woman in Jung's Circle*. NewYork: Simon and Schuster.

Eckermann, J. P. (1836). *Gespräche mit Goethe in den letzten Jahren seines Lebens, 1823–1832*, 2 vols. Leipzig: Brockhaus.

Eissler, K. (1982). *Psychologische Aspekte des Briefwechsels zwischen Freud und Jung*. Stuttgart: Frommann-Holzboog.

Ellenberger, H. (1970a). *The Discovery of the Unconscious: The History and Evolution of Dynamic Psychiatry*. New York: Basic Books.

Ellenberger, H. (1970b). Methodology in writing the history of dynamic psychiatry. In: G. Mora & J. Brand (Eds.), *Psychiatry and its History: Methodological Problems in Research*, (pp. 26–240). Springfield, ILL: Charles Thomas.

Ellenberger, H. (1993). *Beyond the Unconscious: Essays of H. F. Ellenberger in the History of Psychiatry*, M. Micale (Ed.). Princeton: Princeton University Press.

Ellmann, R. (1978)[1988] The life of Sim Botchit. In: *a long the riverrun: Selected Essays*. London: Hamish Hamilton.

Elms, A (1994). The auntification of Jung. In: *Uncovering Lives: The Uneasy Alliance of Biography and Psychology* (chapter 3). New York: Oxford University Press.

Ermarth, M. (Ed.) (1991). *Kurt Wolff: A Portrait in Essays and Letters*. Chicago: University of Chicago Press.

Falzeder, E., Braban, E., & Giampieri-Deutsch, P. (Eds.) (1993). *The Correspondence of Sigmund Freud and Sándor Ferenczi, Volume 1, 1908–1914*, Peter Hoffer (Trans.). Cambridge: Harvard University Press.

Falzeder, E. (1994). My grand-patient, my chief tormentor: a hitherto unnoticed case of Freud's and the consequences. *Psychoanalytic Quarterly*, 63: 297–331.

Falzeder, E. (Ed.) (2002). *The Complete Correspondence between Sigmund Freud and Karl Abraham: 1907–1925, Completed Edition*. London: Karnac.

Findlay, T. (1999)[2001]. *Pilgrim*. London: Faber.

Flournoy, T. (1900/1994). *From India to the Planet Mars: A Case of Multiple Personality with Imaginary Languages*, S. Shamdasani (Ed.), D. Vermilye (Trans.). Princeton: Princeton University Press.

Fordham, M. (1993). *The Making of an Analyst: A Memoir*. London: Free Associations.

Forel, A. (1937). *Out of my Life and Work*. B. Miall (Trans.). New York: Norton.

Freud, S. (1914). On the history of the psycho-analytic movement. *S.E.*, 14. London: Hogarth Press.

Freud, S. (1925). An autobiographical study. *S.E.*, 20. London, Hogarth Press.

Friedman, L. J. (1999). *Identity's Architect: A Biography of Erik H Erikson*. London: Free Association Books.

Graf-Nold, A. (2001). The Zürich School of Psychiatry in theory and practice. Sabina Spielrein's treatment at the Burghölzli clinic in Zürich. *Journal of Analytical Psychology*, 46(1): 73–104.

Hall, G. S. (1923). *Life and Confessions of a Psychologist*. New York: D. Appleton & Co.

Hampton, C. (2002). *The Talking Cure*. London: Faber.

Hannah, B. (1967). Some glimpses of the individuation process in Jung himself. Zürich: mimeographed.

Hannah, B. (1976). *C. G. Jung: His Life and Work. A Biographical Memoir*. New York: Perigree.

Hauke, C. (2000). *Jung and the Postmodern: The Interpretation of Realities*. London: Routledge.

Hayman, R. (1999). *A Life of Jung*. London: Bloomsbury.

Heisig, J. (1979). *Imago Dei: A Study of Jung's Psychology of Religion*. Lewisburg: Bucknell University Press.

Holt, D. (1999). Translating Jung. *Harvest: Journal for Jungian Studies*, 45: 116–124.

Jaffé, A. (1984). Details about C. G. Jung's family. *Spring: An Annual of Archetypal Psychology and Jungian Thought*.

Jones, E. (1955). *Sigmund Freud: Life and Work*, Vol. 2. London: Hogarth Press.

Jones, E. (1959). *Free Associations: Memories of a Psycho-Analyst*. New York: Basic Books.

Jung, C. G. (1917). The psychology of the unconscious processes. In: Constance Long (Ed.), *Collected Papers on Analytical Psychology*, (London, Baillière, Tindall & Cox, 1917, 2nd ed.), pp. 354–444.

Jung, C. G. (1925)[1989]. *Analytical Psychology: Notes of the Seminar given in 1925*. W. McGuire (Ed.), Bollingen Series. Princeton: Princeton University Press/London: Routledge.

Jung, C. G. (1930–1934)[1997]. *Visions: Notes of the Seminar given In 1930–1934*, two volumes. C. Douglas (Ed.), Bollingen Series, Princeton: Princeton University Press.

Jung, C. G. (1932)[1996]. *The Psychology of Kundalini Yoga: Notes of the Seminar given in 1932 by C. G. Jung*, S. Shamdasani (Ed.). Princeton/London: Princeton University Press, Bollingen Series/ Routledge.

Jung, C. G. (1939). *The Integration of the Personality*. S. Dell (Trans.) New York: Farrar & Rhinehart.

Jung, C. G. (1944). *Collected Works*. Sir Herbert Read, Michael Fordham, Gerhard Adler & William McGuire (Eds.), Richard Hull (Trans.). London/Princeton: Routledge/Bollingen Series, Princeton University Press.

Jung, C. G/A. Jaffé, (1962)[1983]. *Memories, Dreams, Reflections*. London: Flamingo.

Kaplan, J. (1994). A culture of biography. *The Yale Review*, 82(4): 1–12.

Kraepelin, E. (1987). *Memoirs*. H. Hippius, G. Peters & D. Ploog (Eds.) in collaboration with P. Hoff & A. Kreuter, C. Wooding-Deane (Trans.). Berlin: Springer-Verlag.

Krell, D. F. (1998). *Contagion: Sexuality, Disease, and Death in German Idealism and Romanticism*, (Bloomington, Indiana University Press).

Lammers, A. (2004). 'Correctio fatuorum'. Re the Jung–White letters. *Journal of Analytical Psychology*, 49.

Lothane, Z. (1999). Tender love and transference: unpublished letters of C. G. Jung and Sabina Spielrein. *International Journal of Psychoanalysis*, 80(6): 1189–1204.

Maillard, C. (1993). *Les Sept Sermons aux Morts de Carl Gustav Jung*. Nancy: Presses Universitaires de Nancy.

McGuire, W. (Ed.) (1974). *The Freud/Jung Letters*. R. Mannheim & R. F. C. Hull (Trans.). Princeton: Princeton University Press; London: Hogarth Press/Routlege & Kegan Paul.

McLynn, F. (1996). *Carl Gustav Jung*, (London, Bantam).

Meier, C. A. (1977)[1995]. *Personality: The Individuation Process in the Light of C. G. Jung's Typology*. D. Roscoe (Trans.). Einsiedeln: Daimon.

Meier, C. A. (1984). *The Psychology of C. G. Jung. Volume 1: The Unconscious in its Empirical Manifestations*. D. Roscoe (Trans.). Boston: Sigo Press.

Meier, C. A. (1989). *The Psychology of Jung Volume 3: Consciousness.* D. Roscoe (Trans.), Boston, Sigo Press.

Muramoto, S. (1987). Completing the memoirs: the passages omitted or transposed in the English and Japanese versions of Jung's autobiography. *Spring: An Annual of Archetypal Psychology and Jungian Thought,* 163–172.

Murchison, C. (1930a)[1960]. *A History of Psychology in Autobiography,* 3 volumes. New York: Russell & Russell.

Murchison, C. (Ed.) (1930b). *Psychologies of 1930.* Worcester, MA: Clark University Press.

Nietzsche, F. (1887)[1969]. *On the Genealogy of Morals.* W. Kaufmann (Trans.). New York: Vintage.

Noll, R. (1994). *The Jung Cult: The Origins of a Charismatic Movement.* Princeton: Princeton University Press.

Noll, R. (1997). *The Aryan Christ: The Secret Life of Carl Jung.* New York: Random House.

Oeri, A. (1935). Ein paar Jugenderinnerungen. In: Psychologischen Club (Ed.), *Die Kulturelle Bedeuntung der Komplexen Psychologie* (pp. 524–528). Berlin: Springer.

Paskauskas, A. (Ed.) (1993). *The Complete Correspondence of Sigmund Freud and Ernest Jones 1908–1939.* Cambridge, MA: Harvard University Press.

Philp, H. L. (1959). *Jung and the Problem of Evil.* New York: R. M. Bride.

Ribi, A. (1999). *Die Suche nach den eigenen Wurzeln: Die Bedeutung von Gnosis, Hermetik und Alchemie für C. G. Jung und Marie-Louise von Franz und deren Einfluss auf das moderne Verständnis dieser Disziplin.* Bern: Peter Lang.

Roazen, P. (1974). *Freud and His Followers.* New York: Knopf.

Robinson, F. (1992). *Love's Story Told: A Life of Henry A. Murray.* Cambridge, MA: Harvard University Press.

Rolfe, E. (1959). *The Intelligent Agnostic's Guide to Christianity.* London: Skeffington.

Rolfe, E. (1989). *Encounter with Jung.* Boston: Sigo Press.

Rowland, S. (1999). *C. G. Jung and Literary Theory: The Challenge from Fiction.* London: Macmillan.

Rowland, S. (2002). *Jung: A Feminist Revision.* Oxford: Polity.

Shamdasani, S. (1990). A woman called Frank. *Spring: A Journal of Archetype and Culture,* 50: 26–56.

Shamdasani, S. (1994). Reading Jung Backwards? The correspondence of Michael Fordham and Richard Hull concerning "The type problem in poetry" in Jung's "Psychological Types". *Spring: A Journal of Archetype and Culture*, 55: 100–127.

Shamdasani, S. (1995). Memories, dreams, omissions. *Spring: Journal of Archetype and Culture*, 57: 115–137.

Shamdasani, S. (1998a). *Cult Fictions: C. G. Jung and the Founding of Analytical Psychology*. London: Routledge.

Shamdasani, S. (1998b). The lost contributions of Maria Moltzer to analytical psychology: two unknown papers. *Spring: Journal of Archetype and Culture*, 64: 103–120.

Shamdasani, S. (2000). Misunderstanding Jung: the afterlife of legends. *Journal of Analytical Psychology*, 45: 459–472.

Shamdasani, S. (2001). "The magical method that works in the dark": C. G. Jung, hypnosis and suggestion. *Journal of Jungian Practice and Theory*, 3: 5–18.

Shamdasani, S. (2003). *Jung and the Making of Modern Psychology: The Dream of a Science*. Cambridge: Cambridge University Press.

Shortland, M., & Yeo, R. (Eds.) (1996). *Telling Lives in Science: Essays on Scientific Biography*. Cambridge: Cambridge University Press.

Smith, R. C. (1997). *The Wounded Jung: Effects of Jung's Relationships on his Life and Work*. Evanston: Northwestern University Press.

Stekel, W. (1950). E. Gutheil (Ed.), *The Autobiography of Wilhelm Stekel: The Life Story of a Pioneer Psychoanalyst*. New York: Liveright.

Stern, P. (1976). *C. G. Jung: The Haunted Prophet*. New York: George Braziller.

Stevens, A. (1990)[1999]. *On Jung*. Princeton: Princeton University Press.

Storr, A. (1997). *Feet of Clay: A Study of Gurus*. London: Fontana.

Sulloway, F. (1979). *Freud, Biologist of the Mind*. New York: Basic Books.

Taylor, E. (1980). Jung and William James. *Spring: A Journal for Archetypal Psychology and Jungian Thought*, 157–169.

Taylor, E. (1996). The new Jung scholarship. *The Psychoanalytic Review*, 83: 547–568.

Vidal, F. (1994). *Piaget before Piaget*. Cambridge, MA: Harvard University Press.

Vidal, F. (2001). Sabina Spielrein, Jean Piaget—going their own ways. *Journal of Analytical Psychology*, 46(1): 139–154.

Von Franz, M.-L. (1975). *C. G. Jung: His Myth in our Time*. W. Kennedy (Trans.). New York: C. G. Jung Foundation.

Wehr, G. (1969). *C. G. Jung im Selbstzeugnissen und Bilddokumenten*. Reinbek bei Hamburg: Rowohlt Raschenbuch Verlag; *An Illustrated Biography of Jung*. M. Kohn (Trans.) [reprinted Boston: Shambala, 1989].

Wehr, G. (1972). *C. G. Jung und Rudof Steiner*. Stuttgart: Klett.

Wehr, G. (1975). *C. G. Jung und das Christentum*. Olten: Walter Verlag.

Wehr, G. (1985). *Jung: A Biography*. Boston: Shamabala, 1988.

West, M. (1983). *The World is Made of Glass*. London: Coronet.

Wilson, C. (1983)[1984]. *C. G. Jung: Lord of the Underworld*. Wellingborough: Aquarian Press.

Wolff, T. (1946)[1990]. A few words on the Psychological Club Zurich since 1939. *Harvest: Journal of the C. G. Jung Analytical Psychology Club*, 36: 113–120.

Wolff, T. (1959)[1981]. *Studien zu C. G. Jungs Psychologie*. Einselden: Daimon.

Wundt, W. (1921). *Erlebtes und Erkanntes* Stuttgart: A. Kröner.

INDEX

"Anna Maria", 78
Abraham, Karl, 72, 92
Adler, Gerhard, 48–51, 57, 58n, 65, 78, 113
Amrouche, Jean, 23n
Aptekmann, Esther, 83
Atmavictu, 99
Augustine, Saint, 17

Bailey, Ruth, 41, 107
Bair, Deirdre, 7, *Jung: A Biography*, 13n, 24n, 33n, 35n, 38n, 48n, 49n, 51n, 60n, 70n, 77n, 87–116
Barrett, Jack, 14, 20, 35–36, 38n, 47, 50, 53, 54n
Baynes, Cary (née de Angulo), 10, 13–15, 18–21, 23, 27, 37, 43, 64–65, 78, 106
Baynes, H. G., 10n, 101, 107, 114, *Mythology of the Soul*, 48n
Beck, Leo, 30
Beckwith, George, 107

Bennet, E. A., 7, 97, *C. G. Jung*, 39–45, 77n, *Conversations with Jung*, 39–41, 42, 45
What Jung Really Said, 44n, "Jung's inner life", 44
Bennet, Eveline, 45
Bishop, Paul, "On the history of analytical psychology: C. G. Jung and Rascher Verlag: Part 2", 52n, 56
Bjerre, Poul, 92–93
Black, Stephen, 19n
Bleuler, Eugen, 17, 54–55, 89
Boddinghaus, Martha, 83
Bollingen Foundation, 14, 47–48, 58
Borch-Jacobsen, Mikkel, 3, 4, 64n
Brody, Daniel, 13, 19, 21
Brome, Vincent, 7, 84, 86, 96, 115, *Jung: Man and Myth*, 74–78, 79n
Browne, Janet, *Darwin*, 118n
Buber, Martin, 50
Burckhardt, Jakob, 17
Burrow, Trigant, 90n

Carus, Carl Gustav, 17
C. G. Jung Biographical Archive, 63–66
Charcot, Jean-Martin, 42
Charet, F-X., 85n
Claparède, Eduoard, 9
Claudel, Paul, *Mémoires improvisés*, 23n
Coleridge, Samuel Taylor, 55
Covington, Coline, "Comment on the Burghölzli hospital records of Sabina Spielrein", 112
Crichton-Miller, Hugh, 31

Dante, *The Divine Comedy*, 103
De Angulo, Jaime, 106
De Angulo, Ximena, 13–14, 47n, 50n
Dodge, Mabel, 106
Douglas, Claire, *Translate this Darkness*, 113
Dubois, Paul, 17

Eckermann, Johann Peter, *Conversations with Goethe*, 22, 23n, 45
Eddington, Arthur, 30
Eisner, Lena Hurwitz, 52
Eissler, Kurt, 64, 66n, *Psychologische Aspekte des Briefwechsels zwischen Freud und Jung*, 72, 76n, 82n
Elijah, 61, 84–85, 99
Ellenberger, Henri, 84, *The Discovery of the Unconscious*, 4n, 66–70, "Methodology in writing the history of dynamic psychiatry", 67, "the notion of the creative illness", 68–69
Ellmann, Richard, "The life of Sim Botchitt", 111n
Elms, Alan, 22n, 38n
Evans, Richard, 19n
Evans-Wentz, Walter, 109

Falzeder, Ernst, "My grand-patient, my chief tormentor: a hitherto unnoticed case of Freud's and the consequences", 91–93
Ferenczi, Sàndor, 72
Fierz, Jürg, 11n
Findlay, Timothy. *Pilgrim*, 1–2, 63n
Flournoy, Henri, 11
Flournoy, Théodore, 11, 30–32, 94
Fordham, Michael, 48–55
Forel, Auguste, *Out of My Life and Work*, 9
Franklin, Cecil, 35
Freeman, John, 19n
Freud, Sigmund, 3, 5, 17, 31–32, 42, 68–69, 72, 75–76, 77n, 82–85, 88–93, 95–96, *The Standard Edition*, 55, 57, "On the history of the psychoanalytic movement", 92
Friedman, Lawrence, *Identity's Architect: A Biography of Erik H Erikson*, 118n
Frobenius, Leo, 30
Froebe-Kapteyn, Olga, 14, 17n

Giacometti, Augusto, 96n
Gillmor, Vaun, 36, 53
Gincburg, Mira, 83
Glover, Alan, 51
God, 33n
Goebbels, Joseph, 30
Goethe, J. W. von, 22–23, 45, *Faust*, 62, 99, 103, "The mysteries", 104
Graf-Nold, Angela, "The Zürich School of Psychiatry in theory and practice. Sabina Spielrein's treatment at the Burghölzli clinic in Zürich", 112n
Gross, Gerald, 29–30, 44

Hall, G. Stanley, *Life and Confessions of a Psychologist*, 9
Hampton, Christopher, *The Talking Cure*, 63, 111–112
Hannah, Barbara, 7, 50, 51n, 70–1, 86, 117, *Jung: His Life and Work:*

A Biographical Memoir, 70–71, 80, "Some glimpses of the individuation process in Jung himself", 70
Hauer, Wilhelm, 109–111
Hauke, Christopher, *Jung and the Postmodern*, 5n
Hayman, Ronald, 7, 88, 96–97, 110n, *A Life of Jung*, 84–86
Heidegger, Martin, 50
Heinrich, Prince, of Prussia, 30
Heisig, James, *Imago Dei: A Study of C. G. Jung's Psychology of Religion*, 68n
Henderson, Joseph, 58n
Hessen, Grossherzog of, 30
Heyer, Gustav, 13
Heyer, Lucy, 7, 13–23, 29
Hinkle, Beatrice, 58n
Hirschfeld, Elfriede, 91
Hitler, Adolf, 30
Hoerni, Ulrich, 33n, 88n, 90n
Holt, David, "Translating Jung", 57n
Honegger, Johann, 62, 89–90
Hull, Richard, 23, 26n, 28, 33n, 35n, 38n, 47n, 48n, 49–53, 54n, 56–57, 58n, 99–100

Jacobi, Jolande, 22, 66n
Jaffé, Aniela, 22–39, 42–43, 53, 57, 62
Janet, Pierre, 17, 68
James, William, 30–32, *The Works of William James*, 55
Jeans, Sir James, 30
Jones, Ernest, 72, *The Life and Work of Sigmund Freud*, 18, 77n, *Free Assocations*, 9
Jung, Andreas, 91n
Jung, C. G. (Titles only). *Collected Works*, 26, 47–58, 88, Abstracts, *Folia neuro-biologica*, 55, "African voyage", 107, *Analytical Psychology*, (1925), 10–11, 14, 60, 97n, 98n,

"Association d'idées familiales", 55, "Attempt at a portrayal of psychoanalytic theory", 91n, *Black Books*, 25, 61, 86, 94–97, 100–1, "Commentary to the *Secret of the Golden Flower*", 109–110, ETH Lectures, 70, "From the earliest experiences of my life", 25–26, "General aspects of psychoanalysis", 93, "Impressions from a trip through India", 25, "Inaugural address at the founding of the C. G. Jung Institute, Zürich", 56, 111, *Modern Man in Search of a Soul*, 50n, "New paths in psychology", 54n, "On the archetypes of the collective unconscious", 56, *Psychology and Alchemy*, 49–50, *The Psychology of the Transference*, 110n, "Seven sermons to the dead", 100–102, *Symbols of Transformations*, 59–60, "Synchronicity," 50–51, 52n, "The family constellation", 55, *The Integration of the Personality*, 50n, *The Psychology of the Unconscious Processes*, 54, *The Red Book*, 25, 37n, 86, 97n, 98–102, 109, 118, "The relation of psychotherapy to the cure of souls", 56, "The structure of the unconscious," 55, "Theoretical reflections on the essence of the psychical", 56, *Transformations and Symbols of the Libido*, 53, 58n, 59–60, 80, 93–94, 99n, 108, "Yoga and the west", 111n, (with Eugen Bleuler), "Komplexe und Krankheitsursachen bei Dementia Praecox", 54–55, Jung/Jaffé, *Memories, Dreams, Reflections*, 22–39, 42–45, 59, 62,

71, 74, 79n, 80, 81–82, 84, 94, 96, 98–102, 107–8, Jung/ Jaffé protocols, 61–62, 84, 88, 94, 96–98, 107–108

Jung, Emma, 19, 62, 82, 91n, 97n, 104, 108

Jung, Franz, 38n, 51n, 76n, 113

Jung-Merker, Lilly, 52

Ka, 99

Kant, Immanuel, 17, 39

Kaplan, Justin, "A culture of biography", 5, 111n

Karrer, Hans, 34

Keller, Alwina von, 13, 25

Kennedy, Emmanuel, 70n

Kerr, John, 85n

Keyserling, Hermann, 31

Kraepelin, Emil, Memoirs, 9

Krell, David Farrell, Contagion: Sexuality, Disease, and Death in German Idealism and Romanticism, 69n

Laing, R. D., 7, Jung and Persons: A Study in Genius and Madness, 78

Lammers, Ann, "'Correctio fatuo-rum.' Re the Jung-White letters", 116n

Lay, Wilfred, 6

Lothane, Zvi, "Tender love and transference: unpublished letters of C. G. Jung and Sabina Spielrein", 112n

Maeder, Alphonse, 65n, 66, 95

Maillard, Christine, Les Sept Sermons aux Morts de Carl Gustav Jung, 102n

McCormick, Edith Rockefeller, 103

McCormick, Harold, 103, 105n

McGuire, William, 38n, 51, 53, 55n, 57, 66n, 86n, 90n, 99

McLynn, Frank, 7, 86, 88, 95–97, Carl Gustav Jung: A Biography, 77n, 81–84

Mead, G. R. S., 100n

Meier, C. A., 71n, The Psychology of C. G. Jung, 55n

Mellon, Mary, 58n

Mellon, Paul, 14–15, 18, 20–21

Micale, Mark, 66n

Miller, Frank, "Some instances of subconscious creative imagination", 93–94

Moltzer, Maria, 83, 96, 104–106

Morgan, Christiana, 112–4

Mountain Lake, (Mirabel, Antonio), 106–107

Muramoto, Shoji, "Completing the Memoirs", 38n

Murchison, Carl, A History of Psychology in Autobiography, 9, Psychologies of 1930, 9n–10

Murray, Henry, 63–64, 66, 113–114

Mussolini, Benito, 30

Nameche, Gene, 7, 25, 28n, 64–66, 88, Jung and Persons: A Study in Genius and Madness, 78–79

"the origins of the C. G. Jung biographical archives", 64–65

Neumann, Erich, 27

Niedieck, Gerda, 38n

Niehus, Marianne, 33n, 35n, 43, 52–53

Niehus, Walter, 34–36, 53

Nietzsche, The Genealogy of Morals, 7n

Noll, Richard, 89, The Jung Cult: Origins of a Charismatic Movement, 104n, The Aryan Christ: The Secret Life of Carl Jung, 104n

Novalis, 68

Oeri, Albert, 30, "Ein paar Jugenderinnerungen", 87

Ovid, Metamorphoses, 62

Paracelsus, 17

Pelet, Emma von, 37

Pfister, Oskar, 66, 92
Philemon, 62, 73, 82, 85, 99
Philemon Foundation, 58n
Philp, Howard, 41–42, *Jung and the Problem of Evil*, 42n
Piaget, Jean, 9
Piper, Leonora, 32
Plato, 17
Plotinus, 17
Poggensee, Emmy, 30, 34

Rascher, Max, 30, 34, 44
Read, Herbert, 23, 29n, 35–36, 38n, 47–51, 53, 58n
Reichstein, Thadeus, "Ueber Alchemie", 110
Ribi, Alfred, *Die Suche nach den eigenen Wurzeln: Die Bedeuntung von Gnosis, Hermetik und Alchemie für C. G. Jung und Marie-Louise von Franz und deren Einfluss auf das moderne Verständnis dieser Disziplin*, 102n
Riklin, Franz (Sr.), 96, 105
Riklin, Franz Jr., 52–53
Rilke, Rainer Maria, 50
Roazen, Paul, *Freud and His Followers*, 77n
Rolfe, Eugene, *The Intelligent Agnostic's Introduction to Christianity*, 109n
Roosevelt, Theodore, 30
Rowland, Susan, *C. G. Jung and Literary Theory*, 5n, 82n, *Jung: A Feminist Revision*, 5n, 85n
Rüf, Elisabeth, 52

Salome, 61, 82, 84, 99
Salomé, Lou Andreas, 82
Sauerlander, Wolfgang, 27, 57
Scheler, Max, 30
Schwyzer, E., 90
Serrano, Miguel, 30
Shortland, Michael, *Telling Lives in Science*, 5

Siegfried, 40, 61, 73, 75–76, 81, 84, 96–97
Sigmund Freud Archives, 64, 66n
Smith, Robert, *The Wounded Jung: Effects of Jung's Relationships on his Life and Work*, 76n
Spielrein, Sabina, 3, 63, 81, 83–85, 96, 111–112
Steiner, Gustave, 11
Stern, Paul, 7, 83–84, 86, *C. G. Jung: The Haunted Prophet*, 72–74
Stern, William, 9
Storr, Anthony, 82, *Feet of Clay: A Study of Gurus*, 73n
Sulloway, Frank, *Freud, Biologist of the Mind*, 4n

Taylor, Eugene, "Jung and William James", 32n, "The new Jung scholarship", 68n
Thorburn, J. M., 12
Toynbee, Arnold, 30

Valéry, Paul, 30
Vidal, Fernando, "Sabina Spielrein, Jean Piaget—going their own ways", 112n, *Piaget before Piaget*, 118n
Von Franz, Marie Louise, 51n

Wadsworth, Cleonie Carroll, 12
Watson, J. B., 9
Wehr, Gerhard, 7, 84, 86, *Carl Gustav Jung: Life, Work, Effect*, 80–81, *C. G. Jung im Selbstzeugnissen und Bilddokumenten*, 80n, *C. G. Jung und Rudof Steiner*, 80, *C. G. Jung und das Christentum*, 80
Werblowsky, Zvi, 48
West, Morris, *The World is Made of Glass*, 62–63, 85n
White, Victor, 116n
Wickes, Frances, 63–64
Wilhelm, Kaiser, 30

Wilhelm, Richard, 17, 32–33, 102,
    109
Wilson, Colin, *C. G. Jung: Lord of
    the Underworld*, 79n
Wolff, Helen, 24n, 26, 34, 36–37
Wolff, Kurt, 22–30, 32, 36–37, 42,
    "On luring away authors",
    22–23
Wolff, Toni, 38, 77, 82, 97n, 101,
    108–110, "A few words on the
    Psychological Club Zurich

since 1939", 110, "Christianity
    within", 110n
Wundt, Wilhelm, *Erlebtes und
    Erkanntes*, 9

Yeo, Richard, *Telling Lives in
    Science*, 5
Young, Stanley, 58n

Zander, Leonie, 52
Zimmer, Heinrich, 17, 30–31